COLLATION, F
STATEMENT OF SIGNING: A WORKBOOK

To Brian McMullin
in friendship and admiration

Collation Reference Notation & Statement of Signing

A WORKBOOK

Carlo Dumontet

THE BIBLIOGRAPHICAL SOCIETY OF AUSTRALIA AND NEW ZEALAND
CANBERRA, ACT
2024

First published in 2024 by
The Bibliographical Society of Australia and New Zealand
Canberra ACT Australia

https://www.bsanz.org/

ISBN: 978-0-6456662-2-9 (paperback)

Layout: Caren Florance, Ampersand Duck.
Typeset in Minion Pro, Skolar Sans Latin and Canto Pen.

Cover: Detail of a watermarked sheet of paper (private collection)

TABLE OF CONTENTS

INTRODUCTION

THIS WORKBOOK WAS BORN OF THE HAND-OUTS I PREPARED FOR A seminar held in 2017. The demand for training in Descriptive Bibliography has always been high among students of bibliography and librarians, and recently I thought that perhaps a practical guide on how to write a collation might prove useful.

The aim of this workbook is to gather together information which is scattered among manuals of bibliography and journal articles and to present it in a didactic fashion. I have kept the text to a minimum and have opted for the greatest possible number of examples. I have explained key points every time they occur in the examples. In doing so I have often repeated myself, but I hope that this repetition will prove useful to readers who will always find the explanation together with the example.

Fredson Bowers's *Principles of Bibliographical Description*[1] contains the most in-depth treatment of the topics covered in this workbook. Bowers based his system largely on that devised by W.W. Greg, first codified in 1934.[2] For this reason, when we refer to the Bowers method, we really ought to say the Greg-Bowers method. The Greg-Bowers method has served the scholarly community well and is universally accepted.

But Bowers's exposition can really try (will try!) the patience of even the most dedicated of students. It needs stamina and determination to get through a text which can be rather obscure and dense. As a personal testimony, I can compare my experience in dealing with Bowers's exposition with Pip's sentiments regarding the alphabet, by paraphrasing his plight:

> Much of my unassisted self, and more by the help of friends than of Mr. Bowers, I struggled through the collation as if it had been a bramble-bush; getting considerably worried and scratched by every letter.[3]

[1] Fredson Bowers, *Principles of Bibliographical Description* (Princeton: Princeton University Press, 1949).
[2] W. W. Greg, 'A Formulary of Collation', *The Library*, 4th ser., 14 (1934), 365–82.
[3] Charles Dickens, *Great Expectations*, Chapter 7 (substituting *friends* for 'Biddy', *Mr. Bowers* for 'Mr. Wopsle's great-aunt', *collation* for 'alphabet').

This workbook has three aims:

- to provide readers with the capacity to construct collations and to interpret published collations (which will vary from bibliographer to bibliographer);
- to explain different techniques of collation-writing;
- to elucidate Bowers's exposition.

The last aim seems to me to be particularly important so that, given the complexity of Bowers's narrative, those who are eager to learn may not get scratched.

The workbook is aimed at students of bibliography and early printed books cataloguers, but I hope that all those engaged in collation-writing may find it a useful reference tool.

When Bowers's, or other scholars', text is quoted I have added in brackets the page number in the source in this fashion: [214 +21] = p. 246, 21st line from top; [200 –16] = p. 200, 16th line from bottom.

> Quotations are boxed, in sans serif, and omissions have not been marked by ellipsis for ease of reading.

Although there is a general agreement on Bowers's method, on several points opinions and practices do vary. In the examples that I have provided (identified by a section number followed by a running number, e.g., §3.1, §3.2, etc.), Bowers's preferred notations are listed first, with alternative solutions following. Explanations are given below each example in this fashion:

» *Bowers (preferred)*: ¶^{4} [2¶]^2 A–V^4.
[Explanation.]

» *Bowers (alternative)*: ¶^{4} π^2 A–V^4.
[Explanation.]

» *Strict prefixed approach:* ¶^{4} χ^2 A–V^4.
[Explanation.]

At various points I have also provided a series of exercises (with blank spaces for the answers) followed by their keys. In the keys, Bowers's preferred method is listed first, followed by alternative methods.

At the end readers will find a *Quick Reference Guide to the Collation*, where only the main points of collation-writing are briefly outlined. In this 'quick guide', some alternatives to Bowers have been provided.

§1 THE FUNCTION OF THE COLLATION

A. *Introducing the collation*

¶ In bibliographical work the collation is a key element in the physical description of a book; its purpose is twofold:

- it informs us on the physical make-up of a book (how it was put together), providing the necessary information for detecting imperfect copies;
- it provides a method of reference to its leaves.

B. *The collation informs us on the physical make-up of a book.*

¶ From a physical point of view, a book consists of one or more folded sheets or part-sheets (sections of sheets), the gatherings, collated (got in the correct order) and joined together by being sewn through the folds at their inner margins. *Figure 1* shows a disbound book of 20 gatherings (top) and the sewing through the fold of a gathering (bottom).

¶ Some of the leaves of each gathering have letters (or signs) and numbers printed in the lower margin. *Figure 2* shows the first leaf of two gatherings of an eighteenth-century book; each gathering bears a letter, i.e., B, C—these are the signatures. After printing, a book would lie in the warehouse in piles of folded or unfolded sheets (*Figure 3*). The signatures helped the printer's warehouseman and the binder to collate the sheets in the correct order.

Figure 1a: The gatherings (folded printed sheets)

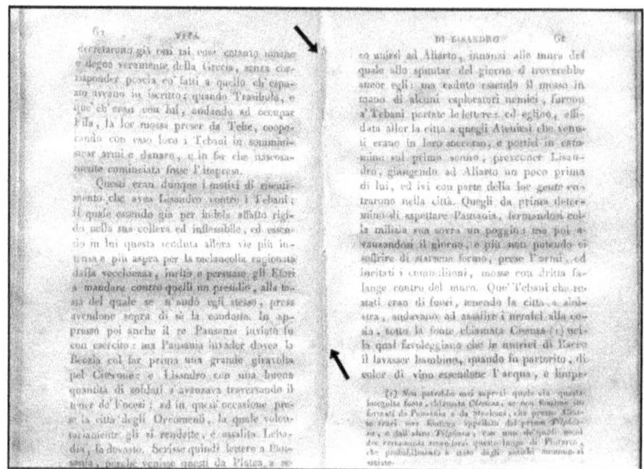

Figure 1b: Sewing through the fold of a gathering

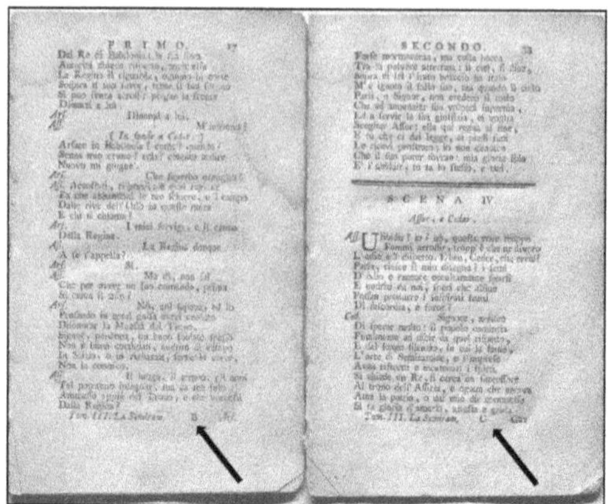

Figure 2: Signatures

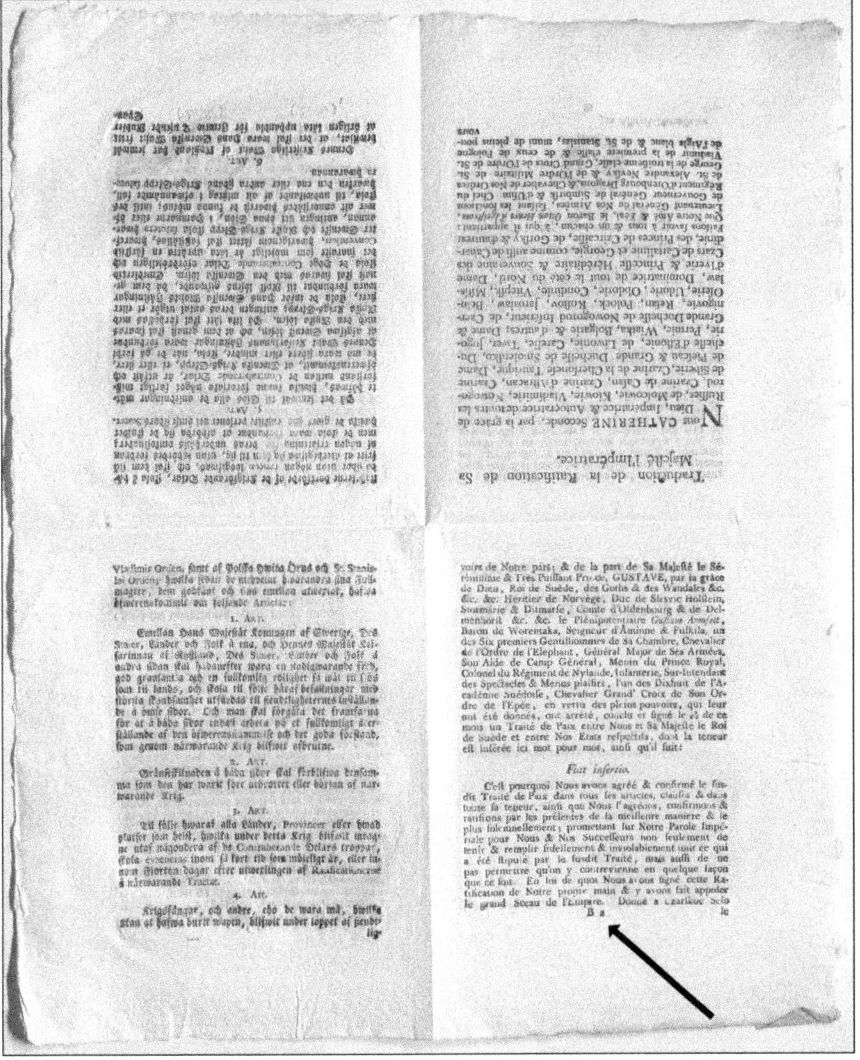

Figure 3: Unfolded printed sheet

¶ The collation records how many gatherings there are in a book, their sequence, and the number of leaves of which each consist of. A collation such as A^4 B–G^8 H^4 immediately and succinctly informs us that the book is made-up of a gathering signed **A** consisting of four leaves, followed by six gatherings of eight leaves each signed sequentially from **B** to **G**, followed by a gathering of four leaves, signed **H**. The collation, therefore, allows us to compare copies of books of the same edition in order to determine any variation from the norm (the ideal copy).[4]

C. *The collation as a system of reference.*

¶ Signatures provide a system of reference. People in the book trades, and book readers, have always referred to book leaves by their signatures, and the same system is used today in bibliographical work. For example, when writing a contents note we need to record the precise location of the different parts of the book, and to do so we employ the system of signatures:

> **A1^r:** Title-page. **A1^v:** Blank. **B1^r:** Text, headed *A letter to a certain eminent British sailor.* **E2^r**: *Postscript.*[5]

¶ Page/folio numbers too can be used for referencing purposes. But many early printed books were not paginated or foliated and, even when they were, pagination and foliation were often incorrect and therefore are unsuitable for reference purposes. While printers took great care in making sure that the signatures were correct, they were less careful with pagination/foliation. That is why signature reference is generally to be preferred.

¶ When writing a collation, the needs of accurate referencing should always be kept in mind. One collational solution may be preferred to another just to avoid ambiguity of reference.

[4] 'An ideal copy is a book which is complete in all its leaves as it ultimately left the printer's shop [...] in the complete state that he considered to represent the final and most perfect state of the book.' (Bowers, p. 113).

[5] This is the contents note for: Henry Bilson-Legge, *A Letter to a Certain Eminent British Sailor* (London: M. Moore, 1746).

§2 A FEW WORDS ABOUT METHODOLOGY

A. *The collation is written according to a conventional system of notation.*

¶ The collation is a conventional system of notation taking advantage of the one already put in place by the printer: the signatures. But although a simple statement such as ‘portrait of the author on leaf B2 recto’ is straightforward and would have been understood by hand-press printers, I doubt whether William and Isaac Jaggard, the printers of the First Folio edition of Shakespeare’s plays, would have made sense of the collation provided for their publication by the Folger Library’s cataloguers:[6]

$^{\pi}$A^{6}($^{\pi}$A1+1 $^{\pi}$A5+1.2) A–2B^{6} 2C^{2} a–g^{6} χ^{2} $^{\chi}$2g^{8} h–v^{6} x^{4} ‘gg3.4’(± ‘gg3’)
¶–2¶^{6} 3¶1 2a–2f^{6} 2g^{2} ‘Gg^{6}’ 2h^{6} 2k–3b^{6}.

This is a highly technical system of notation; no hand-press printer could have fathomed the meaning of the Greek letters **π** and **χ** in this context.

B. *Collation or register of signatures?*

¶ A bibliographical point which has been debated at length is whether or not the collation should report, as much as possible, the exact way in which the leaves of the book are actually signed.

One of the criticisms levelled by Thomas Tanselle at Bowers is that his system of collation-writing seems to be caught between a structural approach (informing us about the physical make-up of a book) and a register of signatures approach (informing us about the way in which the leaves are signed). Tanselle argues that

> The basic purpose of the formula is to show the structure of a book and only incidentally to provide information about signing. Bibliographers still think of the formula as a register of signatures [70 –12].[7]

6 https://folger-main-site-assets.s3.amazonaws.com/uploads/2022/11/Collation_statement.pdf
7 Thomas Tanselle, ‘Title-Page Transcription and Signature Collation Reconsidered’, *Studies in Bibliography*, 38 (1985), 45–81 (pp. 70–71).

This problem is particularly acute when dealing with insertions and many examples of Bowers's and Tanselle's approaches, therefore, will be found in *Section 6*.

§3 NORMAL GATHERINGS

A. *Single signings.*

(a) Signatures, 23-letter alphabet, index numbers.

¶ The printers' system of signatures is based on the classical Latin alphabet, consisting of twenty-three letters:

A B C D E F G H I K L M N O P Q R S T V X Y Z.

This alphabet does not include letters **J**, **U**, or **W**, either in capitals or lower-case. Symbols, such as ✠, †, §, etc. were also widely employed, particularly for the preliminaries.[8]

¶ In the collation superior (superscript) numbers, or index numbers, placed after the signature letter (or symbol) indicate the total number of *conjugate* (or conjunct) leaves in each gathering. Two leaves are said to be conjugate when they form a bifolium, that is, are joined at their inner margins (*Figure 4*). A collation such as $§^2$ $A–E^8$ F^4 means that the book is made up of one gathering of two leaves signed §, five gatherings of eight leaves each signed **A**, **B**, **C**, **D**, **E**, one gathering of four leaves signed **F**.

(b) Letters J, U, and W.

¶ When the letter **U** is used instead of **V**, a typical feature of British printing, no account is taken of this fact in the collation, as we are still dealing with a 23-letter alphabet:

§3.1 A B C D E F G H I K L M N O P Q R S T **U** X Y Z [all in 8s]

» $A–Z^8$.

¶ Rarely the letter **J** is used instead of **I**. Unlike letter **U**, this is an anomaly which may be made explicit in the collation, in spite of the fact that we are still dealing with a 23-letter alphabet. Alternatively, the anomaly may be reported in a paragraph on the typography of the book:

[8] The leaves which precede the actual text, such as half-title, title, list of contents, dedication, preface, etc.

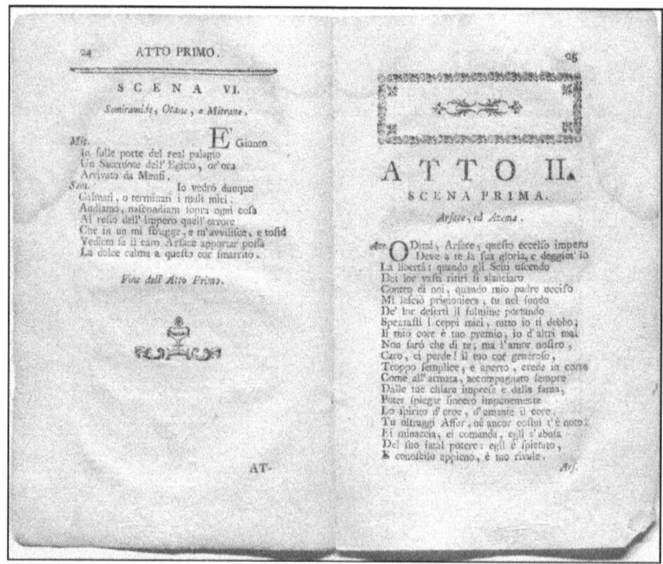

24 ATTO PRIMO.

SCENA VI.

Semiramide, Otane, e Mitrane.

Mit. E' Giunto
In ſulle porte del real palagio
Un Sacerdote dell' Egitto, or' ora
Arrivato da Menfi.
Sem. Io vedrò dunque
Calmati, o terminati i mali miei.
Andiamo, naſcondiam ſopra ogni coſa
Al reſto dell' impero quell' orrore
Che in un mi ſtrugge, e m' avviliſce, e toſto
Vediam ſe il caro Arſace apportar poſſa
La dolce calma a queſto cor ſmarrito.

Fine dell' Atto Primo.

AT-

25

ATTO II.

SCENA PRIMA.

Arſace, ed Azema.

Aze. ODimi, Arſace, queſto eccelſo impero
Deve a te la ſua gloria, e deggio io
La libertà; quando gli Sciti uſcendo
Dai lor vaſti ritiri ſi ſlanciaro
Contro di noi, quando mio padre ucciſo
Mi laſciò prigioniera, tu nel fondo
De' lor deſerti il fulmine portando
Spezzaſti i ceppi miei, tutto io ti debbo;
Il mio core è tuo premio, io d' altri mai
Non farò che di te; ma l' amor noſtro,
Caro, ci perde! il tuo cor generoſo,
Troppo ſemplice, e aperto, crede in corte
Come all' armata, accompagnato ſempre
Dalle tue chiare impreſe e dalla fama,
Poter ſpiegar ſincero impunemente
Lo ſpirito d' eroe, d' amante il core.
Tu oltraggi Aſſur, nè ancor coſtui t' è noto:
Ei minaccia, ei comanda, egli s' abuſa
Del ſuo fatal potere: egli è ſpietato,
E conoſcilo appieno, è tuo rivale.

Arſ.

Figure 4: A bifolium (two conjugate leaves)

§3.2 A B C D E F G H **J** K L [all in 8s]

» A–H⁸ **J**⁸ K–L⁸ *or*

» A–L⁸. *Typography*: signed J for I.

¶ Similarly rare is the use of the letter **W** as an extra letter, making the alphabet a 24-letter one. In this case the anomaly *must* be made explicit in the collation:

§3.3 A B C D E F G H I K L M N O P Q R S T V **W** X Y Z [all in 8s]

» A–V⁸ **W**⁸ X–Z⁸.

¶ In short, the collation A–Z⁸ implies the presence of no letter **W**, and the presence of either letter **I** or **J**, and/or either letter **U** or **V**.

(c) Gatherings signed with numbers.

¶ From the nineteenth century onwards, gatherings were often signed with numbers, instead of letters, although not a usual practice in British printing. Pre-nineteenth-century examples can be found but are rare. In cases such as these the collation will list numbers, not letters:

§3.4 1 2 3 4 5 6 [in 8s] 7 [in 4s]

» 1–6⁸ 7⁴.

(d) Signatures within parentheses or brackets.

¶ Parentheses or brackets printed around signatures are ignored but their presence may be mentioned in a note on the typography of the book:

§3.5 (A)^{4} *or* [A]^{4}

» A^{4}. *Typography:* signatures within parentheses *or*
» A^{4}. *Typography:* signatures within brackets.

¶ In bibliographical work the use of brackets around signatures is reserved for an editorial inference (*Section 4*).

(e) Signatures in different founts and in small capitals.

¶ The collation is set entirely in roman, whatever the fount used in the book. Signatures in lower-case are distinguished from those in capitals. Signatures in small capitals are transcribed as capitals. For example, in:

§3.6 *a*^{4} 𝕬^{4} 𝕭^{4} c^{2}

where two signatures are in Gothic, the first one in italic, and the last one in small caps, the correct notation is:

» a^{4} A–B^{4} C^{2} *not* *a*^{4} 𝕬–𝕭^{4} c^{2} *not* a^{4} A–B^{4} c^{2}.

¶ The presence of signatures in gothic, italic, etc. may be mentioned in a note on the typography of the book.

(f) Sequences of letters.

¶ Unbroken sequences of letters in the same case (upper-case or lower-case) and with the same index number, can be joined with a dash:

§3.7 A^{4} B^{4} C^{4} D^{4}

» A–D^{4}.

¶ When these conditions are not met with, separate sequences are called for. For example, in a situation such as:

§3.8 a^{4} b^{4} c^{4} d^{4} A^{4} B^{4} C^{4} D^{4} E^{4} F^{4}

where all gatherings have four leaves, but the first four are signed with lower-case letters and the others with upper-case ones, two sequences are called for:

» a–d^{4}, A–F^{4}.

N.B. Each sequence must have its own index number to avoid confusion: a–d^4, A–F^4 *not* a–d A–F^4.

Similarly:

§3.9 A^4 B^4 C^4 D^4 E^2 F^4 a^4 b^4 c^4

» A–D^4 E^2 F^4, a–c^4

and:

§3.10 A^4 B^4 D^4 E^4 F^4

» A–B^4 D–F^4.
In this example there is no gathering signed **C**; the sequence must be interrupted to point to the omission.

¶ A regularly alternating sequence of different index numbers can have its own shorthand:

§3.11 A^{12} B^6 C^{12} D^6 E^{12} F^6

» A–F$^{12/6}$ *or* A–F$^{12.6}$.

(g) Arbitrary marks.

¶ Some gatherings, especially preliminary ones, were often signed by the printer with arbitrary marks:

Asterisk: *
Con (Latin abbreviation): **9**
Cross: ✠ (Maltese) ✢ (Greek) ✝ (Latin)
Dagger (also called diesis, obelisk, or obelus): †
Pilcrow (or paragraph (mark): ¶
Rum (Latin abbreviation): **ꝝ ℞**
Section: §

and many more (*Figure 5* illustrates three examples).

¶ Ideally, all symbols ought to be reproduced as they appear in the book for accuracy or so that a close resetting of type may be detected. Many library systems still do not support all symbols, and some must be described in square brackets: [cross]^4 [rum]^4 A^4 B–Y^8. But the problem is: which cross symbol are we dealing with? or which rum symbol?

¶ Arbitrary marks do not belong to any alphabetical sequence and can appear anywhere in a book, as each printer employed them as he thought

QUOD. LAUDABILITER. ET. FELICITER
CONFECTIS. ITINERIBUS
QUAE. AD. LINGUAS. EXCOLENDAS
* 3

m ſingulorum inter ſe nexum ; ſi tranſitiones ab unius
deſcriptionem alterius , ſi perpetuas virtutis propoſitae
tioneſque vitiorum , diligenter conſideres , vix quid-
ſiderabis , ſaltem quid inde reciſum videatur non inve-
que in Epitomen contractus fuerit Valerius , illius ge-
†††
ne-

e tu ? A cui egli riſpoſe. Io ſon
on , che io ti feci , ſono a te tor-
Alquãto ſi ſpauento Meuccio ueg
ſia il ben uenuto fratel mio , &
ꝯ iiii

Figure 5: Symbols: asterisk, cross, Latin abbreviation 'con'

fit. Unless arbitrary marks constitute a sequence, each must be noted by its own index number:

§3.12 ✠ [in 2s] ¶ [in 2s] B–F [in 4s] § [in 4s] G–K [in 4s]

» ✠^{2} ¶^{2} B–F^4 §^{4} G–K^4.

¶ Arbitrary marks were also employed by printers to single out some gatherings or single leaves (singletons),[9] often by adding a symbol to a letter:

§3.13 A [in 2s] B [in 4s] *B [in 4s] C–Z [in 4s]

» A^2 B^4 ***B**^{4} C–Z^4.

In this example, a gathering of 4 leaves has been inserted between gatherings **B** and **C**, and in order to make it uniquely recognizable it is signed ***B** to help the binder to properly assemble the gatherings.

In bibliographical work the asterisk signature is normally rendered by using the asterisk of the standard keyboard (* = Unicode 002A). This character is adequate for signings like ***G**, but unsatisfactory when used on its own, as in *^{4} (a 4-leaf gathering signed *). A viable alternative is the low asterisk (⁎ = Unicode 204E). In a collation these two symbols would respectively look like this:

» A^2 *^{2} B–D^4 *and* A^2 ⁎^{2} B–D^4.

¶ Sometimes offcuts were singled out by marking them with the signature (number or letter) plus a symbol, or just with a symbol. For example, a 12mo gathering may consist of an 8-leaf section inside which a 4-leaf section is

9 Carter so defines a singleton: 'A single leaf, where a conjugate pair would be expected ... A singleton will either be the surviving leaf where the other has been severed for insertion elsewhere, or the severed half in its inset position, or an extra leaf.' (*ABC for Book Collectors*).

inserted (*Figure 6*). If the gathering bore, say, the signature **A**, the first leaf of the *insert* was often signed **A*** or just * (*Figure 7*). This practice would have alerted the binder to the fact that this offcut needed to be inserted in the middle of gathering **A**. These added symbols are ignored in the collation: the notation for this gathering is **A**^{12} (= a 12-leaf gathering signed **A**) and its fifth leaf (marked **A***) is simply referred to as **A5**, not **A*5**.

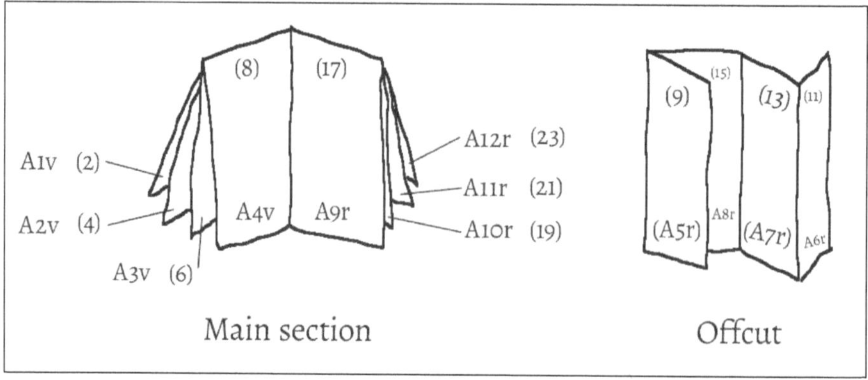

Figure 6: a 4-leaf offcut to be inserted inside an 8-leaf section to form a 12-leaf gathering

coli, e che que sacerdoti che già di concerto passati sarebbero, rigorosa esattezza mostrassero in ogni cosa, e lo interrogassero e lo disaminassero ben bene intorno alla sua nascita, e finalmente poi, facendo mostra
3 *

Figure 7: The first leaf of the offcut of a gathering signed '3' marked with an asterisk

(h) Excursus.

¶ The collation excludes leaves which have not gone through the printing press, such as engravings and etchings (that is, leaves of plates). But one can include separate leaves containing both engraved and printed matter, and engraved leaves conjugate with printed leaves. However, an exception is made for engraved title-leaves and frontispieces. Such leaves are noted at the beginning of the collation in this manner:

» *Bowers*: Engr. tit. + A^{2} B–Y^{4} Z^{2}.

¶ Alternatively, the presence of an engraved title-leaf can be signalled in a note. But an engraved title-leaf *conjugate* with a leaf which contains letterpress is an integral part of the gathering and therefore of the collation:

» [A]^{2} B-Y^{4} Z^{2}. *Contents note*: leaf A1 = engraved title-leaf.

B. *Doubled and other multiple signings.*

¶ If the text extended beyond 23 gatherings the printer doubled, tripled, etc. the signature alphabet in this fashion:

» Aa Bb … Aaa Bbb … Aaaa Bbbb, etc.

Figure 8 shows a somewhat extreme example of this system, a leaf signed **M m m m m m m m**. Doubled, tripled, etc. alphabets are represented in the collation as:

» 2A 2B … 3A 3B … 4A 4B, etc.

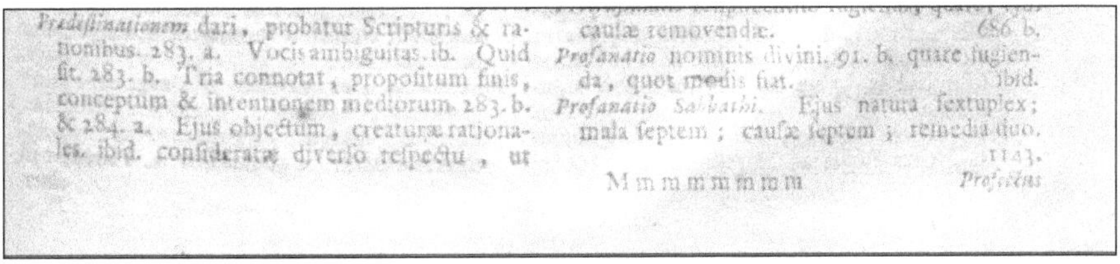
Prædestinationem dari, probatur Scripturis & rationibus. 283. a. Vocis ambiguitas. ib. Quid sit. 283. b. Tria connotat, propositum finis, conceptum & intentionem mediorum. 283. b. & 284. a. Ejus objectum, creaturæ rationales. ibid. considerata diverso respectu, ut

causæ removendæ. 686. b. *Profanatio* nominis divini. 91. b. quare fugienda, quot modis fiat. ibid. *Profanatio Sabbathi*. Ejus natura sextuplex; mala septem; causæ septem; remedia duo. 1143.

M m m m m m m m *Profectus*

Figure 8: Leaf signed M m m m m m m m [= 8M]

In practice the printer was at liberty to use any style he chose, such as an upper-case letter for a second alphabet, and two upper-case letters and one lower-case letter for a third (*Figure 9*).

¶ From the eighteenth-century it became common to sign some, or all, doubled alphabets with a figure and a letter, not **Bb**, **Bbb**, **Bbbb**, etc. but **2B**, **3B**, **4B**, etc. This was a useful device, especially for exceptionally long books, such as collections of legislative material, which, although issued in parts, had continuous pagination and signatures. *Figure 10* shows just such an example.

The signature is **42U** which, in the traditional way, would have been written out as:

Uuuuuuuuuuuuuuuuuuuuuuuuuuuuuuuuuuuuuuuuuu [= 42U]

which is clearly impracticable.

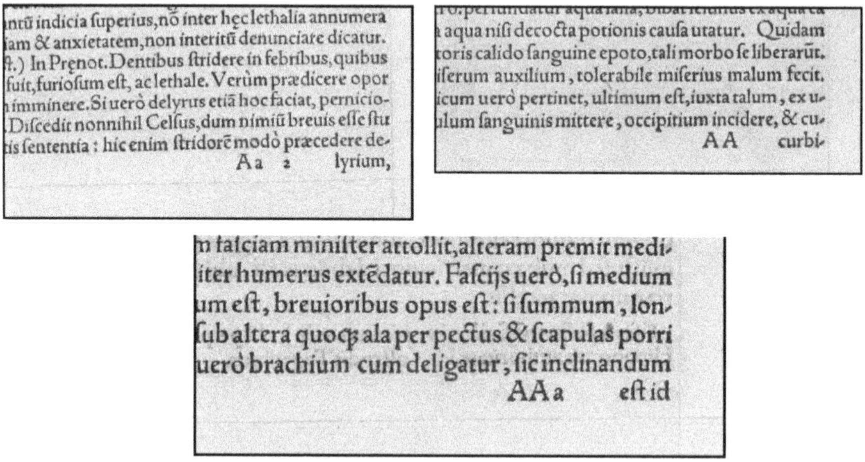
ntū indicia ſuperius,nō inter hęc lethalia annumera
iam & anxietatem,non interitū denunciare dicatur.
t.) In Pręnot. Dentibus ſtridere in febribus,quibus
fuit,furioſum eſt, ac lethale. Verùm prædicere opor
imminere. Si uerò delyrus etiā hoc faciat, pernicio-
Diſcedit nonnihil Celſus,dum nimiū breuis eſſe ſtu
tis ſententia : hic enim ſtridorē modò præcedere de-
Aa 2 lyrium,

aqua niſi decocta potionis cauſa utatur. Quidam
toris calido ſanguine epoto,tali morbo ſe liberarūt.
iſerum auxilium, tolerabile miſerius malum fecit.
icum uerò pertinet, ultimum eſt,iuxta talum, ex u-
ulum ſanguinis mittere, occipitium incidere, & cu-
AA curbi-

n faſciam miniſter attollit,alteram premit medi-
iter humerus extēdatur. Faſcijs uerò,ſi medium
um eſt, breuioribus opus eſt: ſi ſummum, lon-
ſub altera quoq; ala per pectus & ſcapulas porri
uerò brachium cum deligatur, ſic inclinandum
AAa eſt id

Figure 9: Different styles for doubled signings

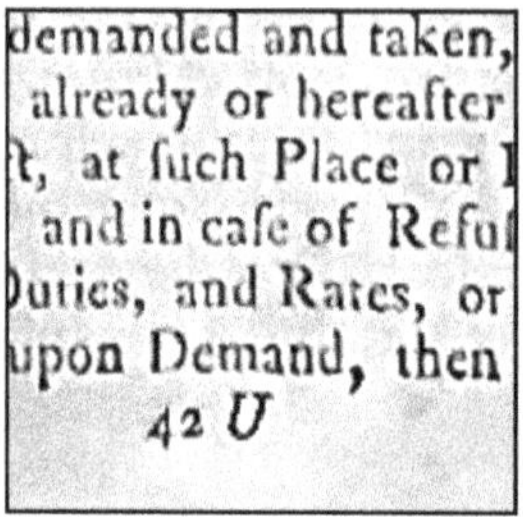
demanded and taken,
already or hereafter
t, at ſuch Place or
and in caſe of Refu
Duties, and Rates, or
upon Demand, then
42 U

Figure 10: Signature 42U

¶ Whatever the style used, the usual formulaic convention holds:

§3.14 A–Z^8 Aa–Mm^8 Nn^4 AAa–BBb^4

» A–Z^8 2A–2M^8 2N^4 3A–3B^4.

¶ The collation can be simplified by joining together uninterrupted alphabetical series sharing the same index number:

» A–2M^8 2N^4 3A–3B^4.

> **N.B.** Signature 2N cannot be joined to the preceding alphabetical series because its index number is 4, not 8. Similarly, it cannot be joined to the following series because there is a break in continuity between 2N and 3A (there are no gatherings 2O–2Z).

¶ Doubled, tripled, etc. arbitrary marks are expressed in the same way as doubled, tripled, etc. letters. A sequence of doubled, tripled, etc. arbitrary marks (of the same type) with the same index number can be expressed by the usual shorthand notation:

§3.15 ¶^{2} ¶¶^{2} ¶¶¶^{2} A–F^4

» ¶–3¶^{2} A–F^4 *or* ¶^{2} 2¶^{2} 3¶^{2} A–F^4.

Sequences of arbitrary marks with different index numbers, as usual, cannot be joined by a dash:

§3.16 ¶^{2} ¶¶^{4} ¶¶¶^{2} A–F^4

» ¶^{2} 2¶^{4} 3¶^{2} A–F^4.

Doubled, tripled, etc. signings accompanied by arbitrary marks are dealt with in this fashion:

» †Ff = †2F.

C. *Duplicated signings of series.*

¶ Whole alphabets can be duplicated, triplicated, etc. in the same book. If there is simply a difference in case between two alphabets (upper-case and lower-case), there is no difficulty:

§3.17 a–c [in 8s] A–V [in 8s]

» a–c^8, A–V^8.

If the alphabets are duplicated in the same case, a prefixed index number is necessary for all duplicated alphabets after the first. The second alphabet is prefixed with the superior figure **2**, the third with **3**, and so on. For example:

§3.18 A–Z^4 Aa–Mm^4 A–Y^4 A–Z^4 Aa–Zz^4

» A–2M^4, ^{2}A–Y^4, ^{3}A–2Z^4.

¶ This collational device is essential for the proper referencing of leaves and pages within each series. A simple statement like 'woodcut on B1^r' could refer to leaf **B1** of any of the three gatherings signed **B**. But a specific statement such as 'woodcut on ^{2}B1^r' uniquely points to gathering **B** of the second alphabetical series.

> **N.B.** The first **Aa** signature does not start a second alphabetical series because it simply continues the signing of the *first* series. Similarly the second **Aa** signature does not start a new alphabetical series but continues the signing of the *third* series. The prefixed index numbers (2 and 3 in this case) serve the whole of their series, and it is not necessary to repeat them. In other words, it is not necessary to write: A–2M^4, ^{2}A–Y^4, ^{3}A–Z^4, ^{3}2A–2Z^4.

D. *Even versus odd index numbers.*

¶ Index numbers ought to indicate the number of regularly quired conjugate leaves in the gatherings. Conjugate leaves in a gathering naturally make up an even number of leaves, and therefore index numbers should always be even. Lack of conjugacy must always be pointed out in a collation. *Figure 11* illustrates the conjugacy of the leaves of a 4-leaf publication (the first leaf is conjugate with the fourth and the second leaf is conjugate with the third).

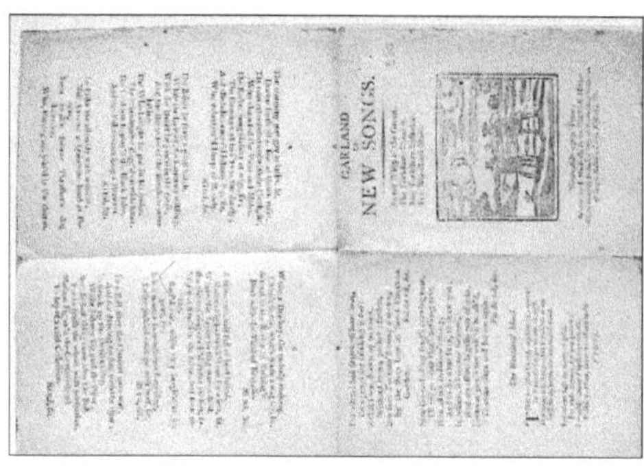

Figure 11: Garland of New Songs of four leaves; unfolded (L) and folded (R)

¶ If a gathering consists of an odd number of leaves, it means that some action has been deliberately performed on it and that one or more leaves have been either excised from or added to it. So, if the second gathering of a book, signed **B**, has only three leaves because the second has been excised by the printer, and is preceded and followed respectively by gatherings of four leaves signed **A** and **C**, one should write

» A^4 B^4(–**B2**) C^4

which precisely indicates which leaf has been excised (this topic will be dealt with in *Section 7*). It would be wrong to write: A^3 B^4 because the notation A^3, although it tells us that one or more leaves have been removed, does not say exactly which ones (*Figure 12, left*).

¶ When we come across a single leaf (a singleton), it is conventional to add a number 1 to the letter or symbol, for example:

» A1

with the number **1** not as an index number (*not* $\mathbf{A^1}$).

¶ But there are exceedingly rare instances when an odd index number is appropriate. For example, some early books were gathered in 3s; there are also books in 18mo format gathered in 9s, an imposition scheme generally employed for short works meant to be bound by side-stitching. The presence of a singleton was no inconvenience to the binder, as the stitching was not done through the folds (*Figure 12, right*).

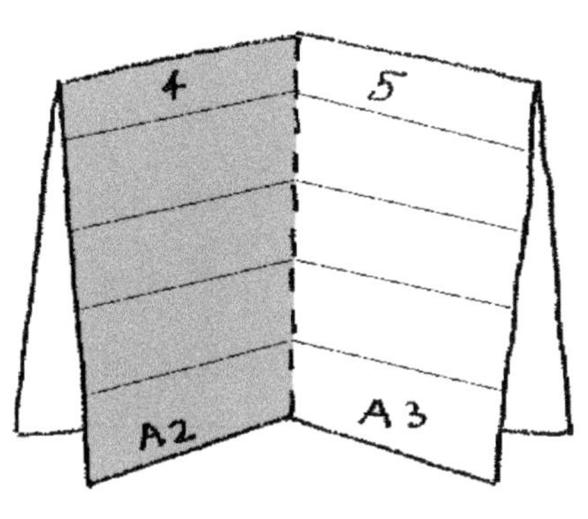

Excised leaf A2

Side-stitched pamphlet

Figure 12

E. *Identifiable misprints, and deliberately incorrect signings.*

¶ Identifiable misprints are silently corrected but are noted in the statement of signing (*Section 8*):

§3.19 A–C^4 C^4 E–H^4

» A–H^4 [$2 signed; misprinting D^4 as C^4].

§3.20 A1 A2 A3 A4 B1 **C2** B3 B4 C1 C2 C3 C4

» A–C^4 [$2 signed; misprinting B2 as C2].

¶ Sometimes the printer deliberately inserted incorrect signings in order to clarify, for the binder's benefit, a printing error or modification. For example, a work may have been planned in several sections, one of which was intended to end with gathering **N**, and the next section to begin with gathering **O** but, owing to a miscalculation, the first section in fact ended with gathering **M**. The printer, to show the binder that nothing was missing textually, might sign the first two leaves of gathering **M** as **M** and **M2**, but the third and fourth as **N** and **N2**. The best option is to treat leaves **N** and **N2** as misprints:

» A–M^4 O–R^4 [$4 signed; misprinting M3,4 as N1,2].

F. *Reference notation.*

(a) General principles.

¶ The system of reference is based on the collation. Whole gatherings are referred to as:

» A^4, B^4, etc.

The first leaf recto of each gathering was normally, but not always, signed only with a letter or symbol without a number. For reference purposes it is customary to add the number **1** to the letter:

» A1, B1, C1, etc.

Leaves after the first are signed, on their rectos, with the same letter or symbol as on the first leaf, followed by a number (arabic or roman): **B2**, **B3**, **B4**, or **Bij**, **Biij**, **Biiij** etc.; **b2**, **b3**, **b4**, etc. or **bij**, **biij**, **biiij**, etc.

¶ In reference, individual leaves, whether signed or not, take suffix numbers in *arabic* (the actual style of numbering may be mentioned in a note on typography). A gathering of four leaves signed **B**, with only *half* of the leaves signed, as is often the case, would have the reference to its leaves given as follows (adding superscript 'r' for the recto of the leaf and superscript 'v' for the verso):

» B1 B2 B3 B4.

» B1^r B1^v, etc.

> **N.B.** Leaves B3 and B4 are not actually signed, but in reference the suffix number indicates the *position* of the leaf within the gathering, regardless of whether or how the leaf has been signed. Title-leaves were never signed, although there are rare exceptions (*Figure 13*).

¶ A full stop between leaf references indicates conjugacy. The reference notation

» A2.3

means that **A2** and **A3** form a bifolium, or two conjugate leaves (*Figure 4*). A comma between leaf references indicates that the leaves are disjunct.

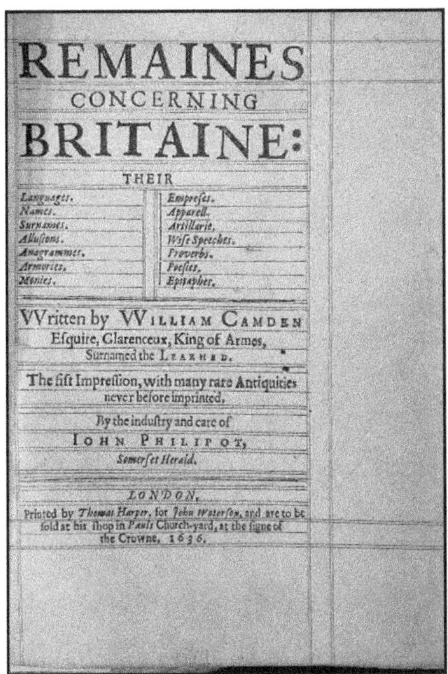
REMAINES
CONCERNING
BRITAINE:
THEIR

Languages.	Empreses.
Names.	Apparell.
Surnames.	Artillarie.
Allusions.	Wise Speeches.
Anagrammes.	Proverbs.
Armories.	Poesies.
Monies.	Epitaphes.

Written by William Camden
Esquire, Clarenceux, King of Armes,
Surnamed the Learned.

The fift Impression, with many rare Antiquities
never before imprinted.

By the industry and care of
Iohn Philipot,
Somerset Herald.

London,
Printed by Thomas Harper, for Iohn Waterson, and are to be
sold at his shop in Pauls Church-yard, at the signe of
the Crowne. 1636.

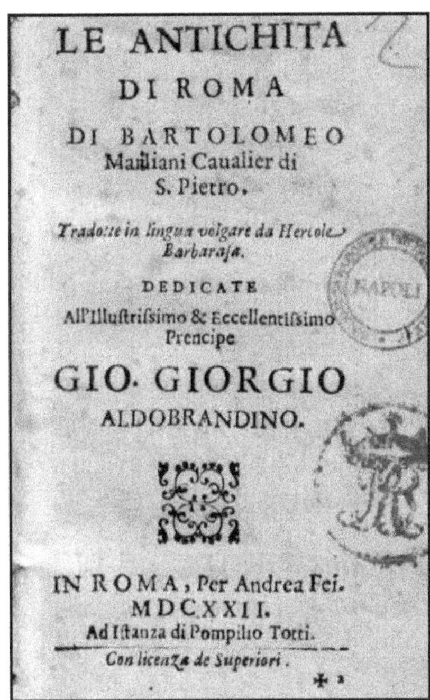
LE ANTICHITA
DI ROMA
DI BARTOLOMEO
Marliani Caualier di
S. Pietro.
Tradotte in lingua volgare da Hercole
Barbarasa.
DEDICATE
All'Illustrissimo & Eccellentissimo
Prencipe
GIO. GIORGIO
ALDOBRANDINO.

IN ROMA, Per Andrea Fei.
MDCXXII.
Ad Istanza di Pompilio Totti.
Con licenza de Superiori.
✠2

Figure 13: Unsigned title-page, and title-page unusually signed (✠2)

The reference notation

» A3,4

means that **A3** and **A4** are not attached at the spine (do not form a bifolium).

(b) Gatherings signed with numbers.

¶ If the book is signed with numbers, the leaf number is given in subscript or in a smaller size. For example, the fourth leaf of a gathering signed **7** is referred to as:

» 7_4 *or* $7{\scriptstyle 4}$.

This is essential to avoid confusion; **A4** is unambiguous, but **74** is not, and 7_4 is the correct notation.

(c) Arbitrary marks.

¶ Arbitrary marks are referred to in the same manner as letters and numbers, but some refinements are desirable. If the collation reads A–B^4 ¶^{2} C–Y^4 and in our bibliographical description we simply say, for example, 'woodcut on ¶1^r', we provide no information about the position of that leaf relative to the sequence of gatherings. To make it easier for readers to immediately locate the leaf, a prefatory superior index with the letter of the gathering *preceding* the symbol may be added to the symbol itself, so that:

» ^{B}¶1^{r}

means that gathering ¶ comes after gathering **B**. Similarly, in the collation A–2B^{4} §^{2} 2C–2Y^{4} the reference to the first leaf of gathering § is

» ^{2B}§1

because the gathering preceding it is signed **2B**.

(d) Sequences other than the first.

¶ In the collation A–L^{4}, ^{2}A–Y^{4} the reference to any leaf of the second sequence must contain a prefixed index number **2**:

» ^{2}A1, ^{2}L4, etc.

There is no need to prefix the first alphabetical sequence with an index number **1**; it is implicit that if no prefixed index number is provided, the referenced leaf belongs to the first alphabetical sequence. Nevertheless, Bowers advocates its use for clarity:

> In the formula A–Y^{4}, ^{2}A–2L^{4} reference to leaf ^{1}B3 beyond all doubt means only leaf B3 of the first single alphabet series and warns that there is another similar series in the book. [258 +18.]

In A–Y^{4} ^{2}A–B^{4} §^{2} C–Y^{4} if we wish to reference one of the leaves of the gathering signed §, which falls within the *second* alphabetical series, two prefixes will be necessary:

» ^{2B}§1, ^{2B}§2

in other words, gathering § is preceded by gathering **B** of the *second* alphabetical series.

Exercise 1

1	¶ ✠.	In 4s.
	a b c d.	In 4s, but **c** in 2s.
	A B C D E F G.	In 4s, but **F** in 2s.
2	¶.	In 2s.
	A B C D E F.	Regularly alternating in 8s and 4s.
3	A → X y Z.	In 8s, but **A** in 6s, and **I** in 2s.
4	A^2 $¶^2$ $✠^2$ $B–Z^8$ $Aa–Pp^8$ $A–Y^8$.	
5	$A–Z^8$ $Aa–Pp^8$ $¶¶^4$ $A–Y^8$.	

Exercise 1 : Key

1 ¶^{4} ✠^{4} a–b^{4} c^{2} d^{4}, A–E^{4} F^{2} G^{4}.

2 ¶^{2} A–F$^{8/4}$ *or* ¶^{2} A–F$^{8.4}$.

3 A^{6} B-H^{8} I^{2} K–X^{8} y^{8} Z^{8}.

Bowers recommends that upper-case and lower-case be always distinguished. Alternatively, one could write:
A^{6} B–H^{8} I^{2} K–Z^{8}.
The argument is that gathering y is part of the alphabetical series A–Z. The fact that it is signed in lower-case is just a printer's mistake. The anomaly will be mentioned in the statement of signing (*Section 8*). The situation in *Exercise 1* is different. There we have a lower-case *series* which is quite distinct from the upper-case *series*.

4 A^{2} ¶^{2} ✠^{2} B–2P^{8}, ^{2}A–Y^{8}.

5 A–2P^{8} 2¶^{4}, ^{2}A–Y^{8} *or* A–2P^{8}, ^{2}2¶^{4} A–Y^{8}.
The problem here is whether to consider gathering 2¶ part of the first or second series. This is usually decided on the basis of contents. The first solution is chosen if 2¶ contains matter belonging to the first series (such as an index); the second, if 2¶ contains matter preliminary to the second series (such as a preface).

§4 INFERRED SIGNINGS

A. *General principles.*

¶ Books may have one or more unsigned gathering. By unsigned gathering Bowers means

> A gathering which has no sign or letter printed on any of its leaves and which has no number used to sign the gathering. Sometimes one or more of the leaves are numbered in the direction-line,[10] even though the letter or sign prefixed to the number is omitted. The presence or absence of direction-numbering has nothing to do with the fact that the gathering is unsigned. [211 -18.]

¶ The signature of leaves left unsigned by the printer can often be inferred. One is safe in inferring signings when the inference completes an alphabetical sequence or when it doubles an arbitrary mark. Inference can be applied to insertions but with limitations (*Section* 6).

¶ Inferred signings are placed within square brackets, with the index number outside the brackets, and are treated as isolated elements within the collation. Some bibliographers prefer to write inferred signatures in italic without employing brackets. This technique can only be successful if the font used has a pronounced slant in the italic. If not, the italic may not be distinguishable from the roman.

¶ Examples of inference in the preliminaries:

§4.1 [unsigned gathering]^4 B–X^4

» *Bowers:* **[A]**^{4} B–X^4.
According to Bowers

> Ordinarily, gathering 'A' is inferred only for the first gathering of a book. [458 -14.]

This is a rather blunt statement, but he further elaborates the point thus:

[10] The *direction-line*, at the foot of the leaf, normally contains both the signature (when present) and the catchword.

> Since normal printer's signing places A either as the initial preliminary gathering of a book, or as the initial text gathering, one should never infer 'A' arbitrarily anywhere in the preliminaries except for the title-gathering or leaf [or a section title-gathering or leaf]. [213 +12.]

There is no general agreement on this point and practices among bibliographers vary. Some examples follow and more will be found in *Section 5*.

§4.2 ¶^{2} [¶1=title-leaf] §^{2} **[unsigned section title-gathering]**^{2} B–M^4.

» *Bowers:* ¶^{2} §^{2} **[A]**^{2} B–M^4.

§4.3 ¶^{2} **[unsigned gathering]**^{2} B–M^4.

The unsigned gathering contains preliminary matter but *not* a title-gathering or a section title-gathering.

» *Bowers (preferred):* ¶^{2} **[2¶]**^{2} B–M^4.
The unsigned gathering is not the first gathering of the book and does not contain the title-leaf or a section title-leaf; therefore it cannot be inferred as **A**. Arbitrary signs too can be inferred when the inference is logical.

» *Bowers (alternative):* ¶^{2} **π**^{2} B–M^4.
Bowers prefers inference to the use of the symbol π for the unsigned gathering (the symbol π will be discussed in *Section 5B*).

» *Structural approach:* ¶^{2} **[A]**^{2} B–M^4.
The fact that the unsigned gathering does not contain a title-leaf, or a section title-leaf, is irrelevant. The main alphabetical sequence starts with **B**, and so we can infer the unsigned gathering as **A**, whatever its contents. This is a valid and unambiguous solution, but is rejected by Bowers.

¶ Examples of inference in the body of the text:

§4.4 B–E^4 **[unsigned gathering]**^{2} G–T^4.

» B–E^4 **[F]**^{2} G–T^4.

The sequence of signatures has a gap between gatherings **E** and **G**, allowing the inference of the missing signature as **F**.
If more than one consecutive signature is inferred, they can be joined with a dash in a shorthand notation:

§4.5 A–D^4 **[unsigned gathering]**^{2} **[unsigned gathering]**^{2} G–T^4.

» A–D^4 **[E–F]**^{2} G–T^4.

N.B. Bowers suggests that inferred sequential signings are better placed within *one* set of brackets. In fact, although **[E]–[F]**^{2} may be unambiguous (and some writers *do* use it), **[E]–[G]**^{2} calls for the assumption that gathering **F** is also unsigned and inferred.

¶ Bowers also warns that:

> It is often dangerous to infer signings of material that has no fixed position in the book. [213 -22.]

Such material includes tables, errata, etc.; often it was the binder who decided where to place it.

§4.6 A–T^4 **[unsigned gathering]**^{4}.

» A–T^4 **χ**^{4}.
This is the conservative approach which, if **χ** does *not* continue the text, may be better than

» A–T^4 [**V**]^4.

The symbols **χ** will be discussed in *Section 5C.*

¶ It is important to remember that inferred gatherings must be treated as isolated elements within the collation in order to avoid confusion:

» [**A**]^4 B–X^4 *not* [**A**]–X^4

otherwise it will not be clear that **A** is the *only* inferred signing and

» ¶^{4} [**2¶**]^4 A–T^4 *not* ¶–[**2¶**]^4 A–T^4.

To quote Bowers:

> The dash can join only similar items in a series, but ¶ and [2¶] are not similar since one is inferred and the other is not. [213 +1.]

B. *Reference notation.*

¶ No special principles apply to inferred signatures. It only needs to be pointed out that in reference the brackets (or italic) are not necessary, since the reference is to location, not signing (or absence of signing). If the collation reads [A]^2 B–F^4 references to the leaves of the inferred gathering will simply be:

» A1, A2.

Exercise 2

1	[unsigned title gathering]^2 ¶^{2} B–C^4 [unsigned gathering]^2 [unsigned gathering]^2 F–Y^4.
2	[unsigned title gathering]^4 [unsigned gathering]^2 C–Y^4.
3	¶^{2} [unsigned gathering]^2 ✠^{2} [unsigned gathering]^2 A–Y^4.
	An alternative solution is possible by using the symbols **π** and **χ** (discussed in *Section 5*).

Exercise 2 : Key

1 [A]^2 ¶^{2} B–C^4 [D–E]^2 F–Y^4.

2 [A]^4 [B]^2 C–Y^4.

3 ¶^{2} [2¶]^2 ✠^{2} [2✠]^2 A–Y^4.

§5 THE SYMBOLS π AND χ

A. *Introducing the symbols π and χ.*

¶ When it is impossible or inadvisable to infer the signature of an unsigned gathering, the Greek letters π and χ are used; π for *prefixed* and χ for *non-prefixed* gatherings.

¶ When W.W. Greg first devised these symbols for collation-writing he thought that π may be appropriate anywhere in the preliminaries and χ anywhere in the text, or body of the book. Later on, he came to the conclusion that the symbol π could be admitted only to *prefixed* gatherings, so that χ could be admitted to *non-prefixed* gatherings, including the preliminaries.

¶ Bowers's definition of *prefixed* gatherings covers a wide spectrum:

> I should be willing to make a very liberal interpretation of prefixed and to assign π to any uninferred and unsigned gathering preceding the first letter, signed or inferential, of the first alphabetical series [whether A, B, C, etc.]; hence if 'A' is duplicated within the same initial series, I should take the second A as the true start of the series. [215 –8.]

¶ There is no general agreement on this point, and according to some writers *prefixed* gatherings are only those which are *prefixed* in the most literal sense, that is, the unsigned and uninferrable gatherings which appear before *any* signed or inferentially signed gathering. In the examples which follow this style of collation writing will be labelled 'Strict prefixed approach'.

> **N.B.** Many writers prefer to identify these gatherings as *prefatory* gatherings rather than *prefixed* ones.

B. *The symbol π.*

¶ A few examples follow.

§5.1 [unsigned gathering]^2 A–D^4.

The unsigned gathering appears before the first signed gathering, which is **A**:

» π^2 A–D^4.

The signing of the unsigned gathering cannot be inferred, as there are no gaps in the alphabetical sequence that can be filled. This is a clear-cut case, and there can be no differences of opinion.

§5.2 **[unsigned gathering]** ^{2} B–X ^{4}.

» *Bowers:* **[A]** ^{2} B–X ^{4}.
Bowers stresses that this unsigned gathering, which is the first gathering of the book, can only be notated by inferring it as **A**.

» *Alternative:* π^2 B–X ^{4}.
This is not a common solution, but it is used by some writers.

§5.3 ¶ ^{4} **[unsigned gathering]** ^{2} A–V ^{4}.

Here the unsigned gathering comes after gathering ¶ and *before the first letter of the first alphabetical series.* We have three options:

» *Bowers (preferred):* ¶ ^{4} **[2¶]** ^{2} A–V ^{4}.
Bowers prefers inference.

» *Bowers (alternative):* ¶ ^{4} π^2 A–V ^{4}.
The unsigned gathering is not inferred but is denoted by the symbol π. Here we follow Bowers's liberal interpretation of *prefixed* gatherings (preceding the first letter of the first alphabetical series).

» *Strict prefixed approach:* ¶ ^{4} χ^2 A–V ^{4}.
The unsigned gathering is not *prefixed* because follows a signed gathering (¶) and therefore must be denoted by the symbol χ.

¶ In the above example **A** is the first letter of the main alphabetical sequence, but this is by no means always the case.

§5.4 **[unsigned title-gathering]** ^{2} ¶ ^{2} **[unsigned gathering]** ^{2} B–Y ^{4}.

In this example we have to deal with two unsigned gatherings which are *not in sequence* (they are respectively found before and after the gathering signed ¶).

» *Bowers (preferred):* **[A]** ^{2} ¶ ^{2} **[2¶]** ^{2} B–Y ^{4}.
Bowers prefers inference. The title-gathering can, and ought to, be inferred as **A**. The signing of the second unsigned gathering can be inferred from the signing of the gathering immediately preceding it (¶).

» *Bowers (allowed):* π^2 ¶ ^{2} **[2¶]** ^{2} B–Y ^{4}.

» *Bowers (allowed):* π^2 ¶ ^{2} $2\pi^2$ B–Y ^{4}.

N.B. In the alternative collations Bowers waves away his rule that the title-gathering ought to be inferred as **A** (*Example §4.1*). The reason given is that, when two unsigned gatherings are *not in sequence*, inferring the title-gathering as **A** may result in ambiguity of reference.

§5.5 [unsigned title-gathering]^4 *^{4} C–X^4.

» *Bowers (preferred):* π^4 *^{4} C–X^4.
It would be improper to infer the unsigned title-gathering as **A** because there is no gathering **B** to connect it with **C**. Similarly, it would be improper to infer the unsigned title-gathering as **B** because the printer would not have signed a title-gathering **B** if there were no actual or inferred **A** gathering.

» *Structural approach:* [**A**]^4 *^{4} C–X^4.
Some writers would find the absence of a gathering signed **B** irrelevant.

» *Alternative:* [**A**]^4 B–X^4.
The actual signing of the second gathering (*) is ignored in favour of the continuity in the alphabetical series but it is reported in the statement of signing: **B1,2 signed *, *2**.

§5.6 [unsigned title-gathering]^2 a–q^4 B–X^4.

¶ In this example the title-gathering (which could be inferred) lies a long way away from gathering **B**, 16 gatherings away to be precise. In cases such as this, Bowers suggests that

> Distance may have an effect on the practicability of inference. [213 –16]

and therefore he makes an exception to his rule of inferring the title-gathering as **A**:

» *Bowers (preferred):* π^2 a–q^4, B–X^4.

» *Bowers (alternative):* [**A**]^2, a–q^4, B–X^4.

C. *The symbol χ.*

¶ A few examples on the use of symbol χ follow.

§5.7 A–B^4 [unsigned gathering]^2 C–K^4.

» A–B^4 χ^2 C–K^4.
The signature of the third gathering cannot be inferred because there is no gap in the alphabetical sequence between **B** and **C**.

¶ This solution is not contentious, but there can be differences of opinion when a *non-prefixed*, unsigned, and uninferrable gathering is found in the preliminaries. For example:

§5.8 **[unsigned title-gathering]**^{2} **[unsigned gathering]**^{4} B–Y^4.

» *Bowers:* **[A]**^{2} χ^4 B–Y^4.
The unsigned title-gathering is inferred as **A** as usual. The second unsigned gathering is part of the preliminaries but is a *non-prefixed* gathering as it comes *after* the first letter (inferred in this case) of the main alphabetical series (**A**). It is for this reason that this unsigned gathering is denoted by the symbol χ and not π.

» *Conservative approach:* π^2 **2**π^4 B–Y^4.
This solution is rejected by Bowers as it

> exhibits an unnecessary, and even incorrect, conservativism. [216 +19.]

§5.9 **[unsigned gathering]**^{4}.

¶ We are dealing here with a single unsigned gathering:
» **[A]**^{4} *not* π^4 *or* χ^4.
The notations π^4 and χ^4 are wrong because the symbol π is reserved for *prefixed*, unsigned, and uninferrable gatherings, and χ for *non-prefixed*, unsigned, and uninferrable ones. In this case there is only *one* gathering; this single gathering cannot strictly be called a *prefixed* or *non-prefixed* one (there are no gatherings preceding or following it), and its signature can be inferred, although only from an appeal to normal practice and not from the item itself (Bowers would argue that if the printer had signed the gathering, he would have signed it **A**). In such instances, some writers would infer numbers: **[1]**^{4}.

§5.10 A–B^4 **[unsigned leaf]** C–K^4.

» A–B^4 **χ1** C–K^4.
The signature of the unsigned leaf cannot be inferred because there is no gap in the alphabetical sequence between **B** and **C**.

More examples of the use of χ for unsigned, *non-prefixed* gatherings will be discussed when dealing with insertions (*Section* 6).

D. *Inference versus π and χ.*

¶ Bowers always prefers inference when attainable. In fact, he warns that:

> The symbol[s] π [and χ] must not be used loosely when the signing of a unit can be inferred with safety and clarity. [214 +16.]

Therefore in:

§5.11 [unsigned gathering]^2 B–M^4

Bowers's preferred notation is

» **[A]**^{2} B–M^4 *not* π^2 B–M^4

and in:

§5.12 A^2 B–D^4 **[unsigned gathering]^2** F–M^4

the correct notation is

» A^2 B–D^4 **[E]**^{2} F–M^4 *not* A^2 B–D^4 χ^2 F–M^4.

E. *Using more than one π or χ symbol.*

¶ If we need to use more than one **π** or χ symbol, we can double, triple, etc. them:

§5.13 [unsigned gathering]^2 [unsigned gathering]^2 A–V^4

» **π–2π^2** A–V^4.

The signing of the first two unsigned gatherings cannot be inferred but, as they are *prefixed* gatherings, we can denote them both with the symbol **π**. To ensure precise referencing, we must distinguish between them, hence the doubling of the second symbol **π**. Furthermore, because they are consecutive and have the same index number, we can link them in a series (**π–2π**^{2}). If we fail to differentiate them a statement like 'woodcut on π2^v' could refer to either of the unsigned gatherings, whereas 'woodcut on 2π2^v' is unequivocal.

§5.14 A–D^4 **[unsigned gathering]^2 [unsigned gathering]^2** E–V^4

» A–D^4 **χ–2χ^2** E–V^4.

¶ It is important not to reference a doubled (tripled, etc.) **π** or **χ** gathering with a superscript prefixed index number:

» A^4 **χ–2χ^2** B–V^4 *not* A^4 **χ^2 ^{2}χ** B–V^4

otherwise the reference, say, to the first leaf of gathering **B** would become ^{2}**B1** instead of just **B1**. Prefixed index numbers are used only to denote duplicated signings (*Section 3C*).

F. *The symbol π as an index symbol.*

¶ When a *prefixed* leaf, gathering, or series of gatherings is repeated by the same system of signing as the main signed ones, the symbol π can be employed to ensure proper referencing. For example:

§5.15 A^4 a–f^4, A–M^8.

In this example we need to distinguish, in reference, the *prefixed* gathering **A** from gathering **A** of the main series:

» *Bowers:* $^{\pi}$**A**^{4} a–f^4, **A**–M^8.
The first gathering **A** is a *prefixed* gathering and so the symbol π can be added to it as an index number. There are no alternatives to this approach.

§5.16 A^4 **a**–d^4 B–Z^4, **a**–$2f^4$.

¶ Here we need to distinguish, in reference, between gatherings **a b c d** of the first lower-case series, from gatherings **a b c d** of the second lower-case series:

» *Bowers:* A^4 $^{\pi}$**a**–d^4 B–Z^4, **a**–$2f^4$.
The first lower-case series (**a–d**) is not a *prefixed* series even by Bowers's own definition ('Any gathering preceding the first letter, signed or inferential, of the first alphabetical series'). The first lower-case series (**a–d**) does *not* precede but *follows* the first letter (**A**) of the first alphabetical series. In cases such as this Bowers suggests further relaxing the rules governing *prefixed* gatherings to include

> Any prefixed partial series which duplicates a main series found later where it would not seem fitting to degrade the later main sequence to the rank of a secondary duplicating series [220 +16.]

adding a warning:

> Clearly this is skating on thin ice. [220 –21.]

» *Alternative:* A^4 **a**–d^4 B–Z^4, ^{2}**a**–$2f^4$.
This solution is favoured by many writers. In fact the instruction 'where it would not seem fitting' in the quote above leaves ample room for manoeuvre.

» *Strict prefixed approach:* A^4 $^{\chi}$**a**–d^4 B–Z^4, a–2f^4.
This approach prefers to 'skate on *thick* ice'. The first lower-case series is not strictly *prefixed*, and so the symbol χ (and not π) must be added to it as an index number.

§5.17 A^2 B^4 C1, A–X^4.

» *Bowers (preferred):* $^{\pi}$**A**^{2} $^{\pi}$**B**^{4} $^{\pi}$**C1**, A–X^4.
The first alphabetical series (**A B C**) is *prefixed* as it comes before the *main* alphabetical series (**A–X**) and so the symbol π can be added to it as a superior index figure.

» *Bowers (alternative):* $^{\pi}$**A**^{2} B^4 C1, A–X^4.
In this example the superscript symbol π is written once to serve the whole series (up to the comma).

§5.18 [unsigned gathering]^4 [unsigned gathering]^2 A–M^4.

» *Bowers:* **π**^{4} **2π**^{2} A–M^4.
The first unsigned gathering cannot be inferred because the main alphabetical sequence begins with an **A**.

G. *The symbol χ as an index symbol*

¶ Leaves or gatherings which are not *prefixed* and bear a signature duplicated elsewhere, must be marked with the symbol χ to ensure precise referencing.

> **N.B.** Duplication can be the result of the failure to dovetail two simultaneously composed parts, or of error.

A few examples follow.

§5.19 A^4 ¶^{2} B–C^4 **D**^{4} **D**^{4} ¶^{2} E–F^4.

» *Bowers:* A^4 ¶^{2} B–C^4 **D**^{4} $^{\chi}$**D**^{4} $^{\chi}$¶^{2} E–F^4.
In cases such as this, the index symbol χ is generally assigned to the *second* gathering when there is indifferent choice. Here we also have two ¶ signings which need differentiating for proper referencing. The symbol χ must be added to the *second* ¶ signing as a superior index.

> **N.B.** The second ¶ gathering cannot be expressed in the collation as 2¶ because it is not signed so (¶¶). Arbitrary marks can be doubled when their signing is inferred (¶^{2} [2¶]^2) (*Example §4.3*).

§5.20 A^4 B–C^4 **[leaf signed D]** D^4 E–F^4.

» *Bowers:* A–C^4 **$^{\chi}$D1 D**–F^4.
Here the first **D** gathering is made-up of an *odd* number of leaves (just one) and therefore it would be better to add the prefixed index χ to it, rather than to the following 4-leaf **D** gathering.

> **N.B.** In this and in the preceding example an index number 2 cannot be used instead of the symbol χ because that technique is used specifically for duplicated signings of series (*Section 3C*). The correct notations are **D^4 $^{\chi}D^4$** *not* **D^4 $^2D^4$** and **$^{\chi}$D1 D–F^4** *not* **D1 ^{2}D4 E–F^4**.

H. *Collections of works.*

¶ In the case of collections of bibliographically distinct works, each with independent signatures and potentially able to be sold individually, Bowers suggests we adopt the following solution:

§5.21 **[First work]** $[A]^2$ B–M^8 ; **[second work]** π^4 A–$2F^8$; **[third work]** π^2 A–S^8.

» *Bowers:* **$[A]^2$** B–M^8, **$^2\pi^4$** A–$2F^8$, **$^3\pi^2$** A–S^8.
The preliminaries to each work are treated individually and not collectively, hence the use of the π symbol rather than the χ symbol. Furthermore, we write $^2\pi^4$ and $^3\pi^4$ *not* **$2\pi^4$** and **$3\pi^4$** because these two π signings are not simply doubled or tripled, but belong to the second and third alphabetical series.

» *Alternative:* **$[A]^2$** B–M^8; **π^4** A–$2F^8$; **π^2** A–S^8.
The different works, separated by semicolons, are regarded as three bibliographically distinct volumes. Some writers would find Bowers's notations $^2\pi^4$ and $^3\pi^2$ un-instinctive, as there is no first occurrence of π.

I. *Reference Notation.*

¶ To refer to the symbols π and χ, and to any segment of a collation having the symbols π and χ as prefixed index symbols, we follow the principles governing arbitrary marks (*Section 3F(c)*). Below are references to individual leaves of the elements in **bold** in the collations:

Collation	References
$\boldsymbol{\pi}$–$\boldsymbol{2\pi^{2}}$ B–D^{4} $\boldsymbol{{}^{\chi}D^{2}}$ E^{2} $\boldsymbol{\chi^{2}}$ F–G^{4}.	π1, π2.
	2π1, 2π2.
	There is no need to be more specific by prefixing in superscript the letter of the preceding gathering (${}^{A}\pi1$) because it is implicit that gatherings signed **π** are *prefixed* gatherings.
	${}^{\chi}D1$, ${}^{\chi}D2$ *or* ${}^{D\chi}D1$, ${}^{D\chi}D2$.
	χ1, χ2 *or* ${}^{E}\chi1$, ${}^{E}\chi2$.
A^{2} $\boldsymbol{\chi^{2}}$ B–C^{2}.	χ1, χ2 *or* ${}^{A}\chi1$, ${}^{A}\chi2$.
A^{2} $\boldsymbol{{}^{\chi}A^{2}}$ B–C^{2}.	${}^{\chi}A1$, ${}^{\chi}A2$ *or* ${}^{A\chi}A1$, ${}^{A\chi}A2$.
A–H^{4} **χ1** I–M^{4} **2χ1** N–S^{4}, ^{2}A–K^{4} **3χ1** L–Y^{4}.	χ1 *or* ${}^{H}\chi1$.
	2χ1 *or* ${}^{M}2\chi1$.
	3χ1 *or* ${}^{2K}3\chi1$.
$[A]^{2}$ B–M^{8}, $\boldsymbol{{}^{2}\pi^{2}}$ A–2F^{8}, $\boldsymbol{{}^{3}\pi^{2}}$ A–S^{8}.	${}^{2}\pi1$, ${}^{2}\pi2$.
	${}^{3}\pi1$, ${}^{3}\pi2$.

Exercise 3

1	[unsigned title-gathering]^4 ¶^{4} [unsigned gathering]^4 B–K^8.
2	A^2 [unsigned gathering]^2 a–b^2 [unsigned gathering]^2 A–Y^4 a–x^4.
3	[unsigned title-gathering]^2 a–b^2 [unsigned gathering]^2 B–D^4 [unsigned gathering]^2 E–Y^4 a–x^4.
4	a–b^2 [unsigned gathering]^2 A–S^4 [unsigned gathering]^2 [unsigned gathering]^2 a–x^4.

Exercise 3 : Key

1 *Bowers (preferred)*: $[A]^4$ $\P^4$ $[2\P]^4$ $B\text{–}K^8$.
Bowers's preference for inference, especially the inference of the title-gathering as **A**.

Bowers (alternatives): π^4 $\P^4$ $[2\P]^4$ $B\text{–}K^8$ *or* π^4 $\P^4$ $2\pi^4$ $B\text{–}K^8$
Structural approach: π^4 $\P^4$, $[A]^4$ $B\text{–}K^8$.
Strict prefixed approach: π^4 $\P^4$ χ^4, $B\text{–}K^8$.
This is a rather conservative solution.

2 *Bowers (preferred)*: $^{\pi}A^2$ $[^{\pi}B]^2$ $^{\pi}a\text{–}b^2$ $[^{\pi}c]^2$, $A\text{–}Y^4$, $a\text{–}x^4$.
Bowers's *skating on thin ice*. The $a\text{–}b^2$ series and the unsigned gathering immediately following it are not strictly *prefixed* gatherings even if they are part of the preliminaries. Also, Bowers's preference for inference.

Bowers (alternative): $^{\pi}A^2$ $[B]^2$ $a\text{–}b^2$ $[c]^2$; $A\text{–}Y^4$, $a\text{–}x^4$.

The first superscript π serves the whole prefixed series.

Bowers (alternative): $^{\pi}A^2$ π^2 $^{\pi}a\text{–}b^2$ $2\pi^2$; $A\text{–}Y^4$, $a\text{–}x^4$.
No inference.

Strict prefixed approach: $^{\pi}A^2$ χ^2 $^{\chi}a\text{–}b^2$ $2\chi^2$, $A\text{–}Y^4$, $a\text{–}x^4$.
A very conservative solution.

3 *Bowers (preferred):* $[A]^2$ $^{\pi}a\text{–}b^2$ $[^{\pi}c]^2$, $B\text{–}D^4$ χ^2 $E\text{–}Y^4$, $a\text{–}x^4$.
Bowers's *skating on thin ice* and his preference for inference.
Bowers (alternative): $[A]^2$ $^{\pi}a\text{–}b^2$ π^2, $B\text{–}D^4$ χ^2 $E\text{–}Y^4$, $a\text{–}x^4$.
Structural approach: π^2 $^{\pi}a\text{–}b^2$, $[A]^2$ $B\text{–}D^4$ χ^2 $E\text{–}Y^4$, $a\text{–}x^4$.
The second unsigned gathering is inferred as **A** even if it is not the title-gathering.

Alternative: $[A]^2$ $a\text{–}b^2$ $[c]^2$, $B\text{–}D^4$ χ^2 $E\text{–}Y^4$, $^{2}a\text{–}x^4$.
Many writers would find acceptable treating the main alphabetical sequence (a–x) as a 'secondary' one. Variations on this solution are possible.

4 *Bowers (preferred):* $^{\pi}a\text{–}b^2$ $[^{\pi}c]^2$, $A\text{–}S^4$ $[T\text{–}V]^2$, $a\text{–}x^4$.
Inference throughout.

Bowers (alternative): $^{\pi}a\text{–}b^2$ π^2, $A\text{–}S^4$ $\chi\text{–}2\chi^2$, $a\text{–}x^4$.
No inference.

Strictly prefixed approach: $^{\pi}a\text{–}b^2$ χ^2, $A\text{–}S^4$ $2\chi\text{–}3\chi^2$, $a\text{–}x^4$.
Inference rejected.

Alternative: a–b^2 $[c]^2$, A–S^4 $[T–V]^2$, ^2a–x^4.

Many writers would find acceptable treating the main alphabetical sequence (a–x) as a ‘secondary’ one.

§6 INSERTIONS

Introduction.

¶ *Insertions* are extra leaves which might be added to gatherings of normal conjugacy; these additions may occur between gatherings or within gatherings and may or may not be signed in some way.

It may be useful to mention here at the outset an important point made by Bowers which, unfortunately, is buried in a very long 'Note' in small type and is easily missed. The point concerns inference, and warns us to be cautious in its use *when dealing with insertions*:

> Inference in signing is not of crucial importance in the collational formula, and when it is adopted, the reason is usually one of superior convenience for reference. Inference, therefore, is made only conservatively and on sufficient evidence. [246 +19.]

Bowers distinguishes four types of insertion and two sub-types for each:

- Separate (disjunct) leaves *outside* or *inside* the gathering (*associated* or *not associated* with the preceding or following gathering).
- Folds *outside* or *inside* the gathering (*associated* or *not associated* with the preceding or following gathering).

There is no general agreement on this 'classification'. Some writers argue that only leaves *within* the gathering can truly be called insertions and that it is hard to view anything *between* gatherings as such.

¶ Thomas Tanselle, in particular, proposes a purely structural approach to dealing with insertions, shifting the focus from the actual signings of the insertions to their position and relation with adjacent signed leaves. Tanselle's notations simply employ the plus sign followed by digits: **+1** = + 1 leaf ; **+1,2** = + two disjunct leaves ; **+1.2** = + two conjugate leaves, etc. These notations indicate position only, not signings, whether actual or inferred. Signatures are not reported in the collation but are recorded in the statement of signing instead:

> The other direction one could go is not to attempt at all to report actual signatures of leaves within parentheses. The information provided would

> then be purely structural, the details of signing to be reported separately. [74 +1.]

In this way, Bowers's complex rules on when to quote or not to quote the actual signature of the insertion, can be completely dispensed with.

Tanselle provides only examples on how to deal with insertions *inside* the gathering. I assume, therefore, that he substantially agrees with Bowers on how to deal with insertions *outside* the gathering, except regarding the use of the symbol χ within parentheses (*Example* §6.2). The examples that follow, I hope, will make these points clear.

A. *Separate (disjunct) leaves outside the gathering.*

(a) Not associated with the preceding or following gathering.

¶ According to Bowers

> In most circumstances it is advisable to treat an unsigned leaf, fold, or series of leaves between gatherings as a separate item. [236 –18.]

and

> If these [separate] leaves [outside the gathering] are unsigned, or if signed with some arbitrary mark not associated with the adjoining gatherings, or if signed as a separate item in a consecutive series, they may be treated in the collation as separate items. [235 –4.]

There is a general agreement on this point, although different approaches to the collation-writing. A few examples:

§6.1 A–C^{4} ¶ **¶2** D–K^{4}.

A *series* of two leaves, respectively signed ¶ and **¶2**, are inserted between gathering **C** and **D**.

» *Bowers:* A–C^{4} **¶1,2** D–K^{4}.
There are no alternatives to this approach.

N.B. The notation **¶1,2** (and similar ones) could also be expressed as **¶1,¶2**. Bowers seems to suggest that the choice depends on whether there is a need for absolute clarity or not. The notation **¶1,2** does not pose problems of interpretation and is Bowers's choice, but the same cannot be said of **C**^{4}**(C4+'C5',6,7)** and Bowers's preferred notation is C^{4}**(C4+'C5',C6,C7)** (*Example §6.7*). On the other hand, **D4(D4+*D4.5.6)** is acceptable because, according to Bowers, with folds there is less need to be precise about the inferred signing of unsigned leaves (*Example §6.19*).

§6.2 A–C^{4} **[unsigned leaf]** D–L^{4} **[unsigned leaf]** N–P^{4} **[unsigned leaf].**

» *Bowers (preferred):* A–C^{4} **χ1** D–L^{4} **[M]1** N–P^{4} **2χ1**.
Here there is no evidence for associating the first unsigned leaf with either gathering **C** or **D**, and the third unsigned leaf with gathering **P**. The second unsigned leaf can be inferred as **M** because there is a gap in the alphabetical sequence between **L** and **N**. If the text were continuous, the final leaf could be inferred as **Q1**.

» *Bowers (alternative):* A–B^{4} C^{4}**(C4+χ1)** D–L^{4} **[M]1** N–P^{4} **χ1** *or* A–B^{4} C^{4}**(C4+1)** D–L^{4} **[M]1** N–P^{4} **χ1**.
These are Bowers's association solutions (expressed positionally) allowed

> on simple grounds of convenience for reference. [236 +12.]

Tanselle objects to the use of the symbol χ, within parenthesis, for insertions:

> Choosing "χ" for an unsigned inserted leaf or fold [as in C4(C4+χ1)] seems inappropriate, because it is treating an insertion in a gathering as it were an independent gathering. Some such symbol as "χ" is needed for an unsigned and uninferrable gathering, but for an unsigned insertion within a gathering no signature is required, since the leaf or leaves take their identity from the gathering itself. [Tanselle, 72 +9.]

§6.3 A–C^{4} **[unsigned leaf] [unsigned leaf]** D^{4}.

Here we have two unsigned disjunct leaves inserted between gathering **C** and **D**.

» *Bowers (preferred):* A–C^{4} **χ1 2χ1** D^{4}.
The signature of the two unsigned leaves cannot be inferred because there is no gap in the alphabetical sequence.

N.B. The correct notation is A–C^4 **χ1** 2χ1 D^4 *not* A–C^4 **χ1,2** D^4. Two unsigned leaves can be written as **χ1,2** only when they are insertions within parentheses as in C^4(C4+**χ1,2**), the comma being a shorthand for *disjunct* leaves. This is allowed because the notation is positional, meaning 'after C4 come two unsigned disjunct leaves'. In reference the first leaf is **C(χ1)** *not* **χ1** and the second is **C(χ2)** *not* **2χ1**. If not insertions within parentheses, the two disjunct leaves ought to be reported as two different units: **χ1** and **2χ1**, which would also be their reference notations. In order to deal with two unsigned and uninferrable disjunct leaves, *we* assign them the χ signature, but that does not make them belong to the same gathering; one belongs to the χ gathering, and the other to the **2χ** gathering: two different gatherings, as different as **A** and **B**. On the other hand, if the two disjunct leaves had been signed, say, ¶ and ¶2, the notations ¶1,2 or ¶1,¶2 would be appropriate.

» *Bowers (alternative):* A–B^4 C^4(**C4+χ1,2**) D^4

» *Bowers (alternative)*: A–B^4 C^4(**C4+2**) D^4 *or* A–B^4 C^4(**C4+1,2**) D^4.

This, and the preceding example, are Bowers's association solutions (expressed positionally).

N.B. The notation **+2** can only be used for *disjunct* leaves. If those two leaves were conjugate, the positional notation would be **+1.2** (*Section 6(B)*).

(b) Associated in signing or direction-numbering with the preceding gathering.

According to Bowers

> A single leaf or disjunct leaves at the end of a gathering are considered to belong to the gathering only when they are associated in their signing or direction-numbering with the preceding gathering. [235 -9.]

and

> It is not customary to associate a final unsigned leaf or leaves [with the preceding gathering]. [236 +14.]

These insertions are indicated, within parentheses, by:

- The signature of the final leaf of the preceding gathering.
- A plus sign.
- The signature, or inferred signature, of the interpolation.

For example, the insertion of a leaf signed **C5** after the regular **C4**, is expressed in this fashion:

» A–B^4 C^4(**C4+C5**) D^4.

In cases such as this Bowers insists on association. He argues that

> The formula is clearest when it follows the original printer's attempt to associate gatherings. [241 -16.]

The three main points to remember for this type of insertion are:

- The gathering with which the insertion is associated must be dealt with as a separate unit (that is, by isolating it) and not as part of a series: **C**[4]**(C4+C5)**.
- It is not necessary to know whether the leaf preceding the insertion is signed or not (in our case leaf **C4**). No statement is necessary to that effect (that is, quoting), as the collational purpose of that leaf is purely positional, it tells us at which point the extra leaf or leaves have been inserted. The statement of signing (*Section 8*) will make it clear whether this leaf **C4** is signed or not.
- It is the signature or direction-number of the insertion which points to association.

¶ As it has been stated in the *Introduction* to this Section, some writers argue that only leaves *within* the gathering can truly be called insertions. Brian McMullin, states that:

> A special form of insertion involves the addition of a leaf or leaves outside a gathering but associated with the preceding gathering (or occasionally with the following gathering) by virtue of the form of their signing. Bowers simply regards such leaves as *insertions*, but it may be easier to understand their function if they were considered as *extensions*.[11]

The alternative to Bowers's approach is to regard disjunct leaves at the end of a gathering as not associated with the preceding gathering, whatever their signing. Such leaves are treated in the collation as separate elements. But in order to achieve this in a workable and consistent way, it is better to retain only the signature letter of the inserts and not their signature number.

¶ Some examples:

§6.4 A–C[4] **C5** D[4].

» *Bowers:* A–B[4] C[4]**(C4+C5)** D[4].
Here we have an insertion which, being signed **C5**, is associated to gathering **C**. In simple cases such as this Bowers does away with quoting:

[11] Personal communication to the author (9 July 2022).

When there is simple insertion of a disjunct leaf, the insertion is signed as stated in the formula even though quotations marks are not used. [237 -6.]

The leaf is uniquely signed **C5** and there can be no confusion with other signatures; the convention, therefore, is that C4(C4+**C5**) would not be written unless **C5** were actually signed **'C5'**. But many writers, for clarity's sake, in this, as in all other examples in this section, prefer to quote any insertion which is actually signed.

» *Positional alternative:* A–B^4 C^4(**C4+1**) D^4.
The extra leaf *is* associated with gathering **C**, and its actual signing (replaced by the positional indicator **+1**) is reported in the statement of signing: **C(C4+1)** signed **C5**.

» *No association:* A–C^4 $^{\chi}$**C1** D^4.
Leaf **C5** is not associated with gathering **C** and is treated in the collation as a *non-prefixed* leaf bearing a signature duplicated elsewhere (*Section 5G*). The actual signing of the insertion is reported in the statement of signing: $^{\chi}$**C1** signed **C5**.

§6.5 A–C^4 *C5 D^4.

» *Bowers:* A–B^4 C^4(**C4+*C5**) D^4.
Although the insertion is signed ***C5** and not just **C5**, it is nevertheless associated with gathering **C**. Quoting the insertion is not strictly necessary, because its signing is unique, but it may add to clarity.

» *Positional alternative:* A–B^4 C^4(**C4+1**) D^4.
The inserted leaf is associated with gathering **C** but its actual signing (replaced by the positional indicator **+1**) is reported in the statement of signing: **C**(**C4+1**) signed ***C5**.

» *No association:* A–C^4 $^{\chi}$**C1** D^4.
Leaf ***C5** is not associated with gathering **C** and is treated in the collation as a non-prefixed leaf bearing a signature duplicated elsewhere (*Section 5G*). The actual signing of the insertion is reported in the statement of signing: $^{\chi}$**C1** signed ***C5**.

§6.6 A–C^4 5 D^4.

» *Bowers:* A–B^4 C^4(**C4+'5'**) D^4.
The insertion is only direction-numbered **5** but it is still associated with gathering **C**. It is necessary to quote the insertion because its signing is anomalous. Quotes also obviate the suggestion that **5** may mean five disjunct leaves.

» *Positional alternative:* A–B^4 C^4(**C4+1**) D^4.
The inserted leaf is associated with gathering **C** but its actual signing (replaced by the positional indicator **+1**), is reported in the statement of signing: **C(C4+1)** direction-numbered **5**.

» *No association:* A–C^4 **χ1** D^4.
The insertion can only be treated as unsigned (**χ1**) because the leaf bears no signature but just the direction-number **5**, which is reported in the statement of signing: ^{C}**χ1** signed **5**.

§6.7 A–C^4 **C5** **[unsigned leaf]** **[unsigned leaf]** D^4.

» *Bowers (preferred):* A–B^4 C^4(**C4+'C5',C6,C7**) D^4.
The first inserted leaf is signed **C5** and so we can associate it with gathering **C**. The question is whether the two following unsigned leaves can be inferred or not. Bowers's guidelines are:

> If a signed insert is appended to a gathering and in turn is followed by an unsigned disjunct leaf [or leaves], the relation of these inserted leaves may be indicated by inference. [237 –15.]

and

> In ordinary usage the formulary admits inference **only if there is some peg to hang it on**. [249 –15.]

This last point is an important one. Here the signed leaf **C5** provides the peg on which to hang the inference of the following unsigned leaves. Therefore, according to Bowers,

> An inferential signing is shown by the absence of quotation in connection with a quoted signature. [237 –4.]

and

> [The inference of unsigned leaves following a signed insertion] is natural and generally desirable because of the[ir] ultimate and unambiguous position. [239 –12.]

So, the fact that one insertion is in quotes means that it is signed, whereas the fact that the two insertions immediately following it are not in quotes means that they are inferred. This is permitted because the unsigned insertions *follow* the signed one; that is, their position is 'ultimate and unambiguous' and will not pose referencing problems.

The commas separating the inserted leaves indicate that they are disjunct (**'C5',C6,C7**).

» *Bowers (alternative):* A–B^4 C^4(**C4+'C5',χ1,2**) D^4.
The two unsigned insertions are left uninferred.

» *Bowers (alternative):* A–B^4 C^4(**C4+C5+2**) D^4.
With Bowers's method, the positional notation **+2** can be applied only to unsigned *disjunct* leaves.

» *Positional alternative*: A–B^4 C^4(**C4+3**) D^4.
The inserted leaves are associated with gathering **C** but the actual signing is reported in the statement of signing: **C(C4+1)** signed **C5**.

» *No association*: A–B^4 C^4 $^{\chi}$**C1** **χ1** **2χ1** D^4.
Leaf **C5** is not associated with gathering **C** and is treated in the collation as a non-prefixed leaf bearing a signature duplicated elsewhere *(Section 5G)*. The actual signing of the insertion is reported in the statement of signing: $^{\chi}$**C1** signed **C5**.

§6.8 A–B^4 C^6 **¶4** D–F^4 G^2 **¶G** H–K^4.

» *Bowers:* A–B^4 C^6(**C6+'¶4'**) D–F^4 G^2 ¶G1 H–K^4.
The inserted **¶4** is associated with gathering **C** on the basis of its direction-number, even if its signing has a different symbol (¶) and its direction number is **4** and not **7**: the simple presence of a direction-number prompts association with the preceding gathering. The second insertion (**¶G**) is signed with a presumed **1** and therefore it cannot be associated with the previous gathering but must be treated as a separate element. Bowers states that

> A number would be assigned the first leaf of any signing [for reference purposes] [237 +12]

hence **¶G1**.

» *Positional alternative*: A–B^4 C^6(**C6+1**) G^2 **¶G1** H–K^4.
Leaf **¶4** is associated with gathering **C** but its actual signing (replaced by the positional indicator **+1**) is reported in the statement of signing: **C(C6+1)** signed **¶4**.

» *No association:* A–B^4 C^6 ¶1 D–F^4 G^2 ¶G1 H–K^4.
Leaf **¶4** is not associated with gathering **C** and is treated in the collation as a separate element. Its actual signing is reported in the statement of signing: **¶1** signed **¶4**.

(c) Insertions ‘associated’ in signing or direction-numbering with the following gathering.

¶ Bowers suggests treating these types of insertion as ‘not associated’:

§6.9 A–C^4 **D** D–E^4.

» *Bowers:* A–C^4 $^{\chi}$**D1** D^4 E^4.
There is practically a universal agreement on this point.

» *Alternative:* A–C^4 D^4(**‘D1’+D1**) E^4.
The alternative is to quote the signing of the interpolation to distinguish it from the regular **D1** signing, and to inform readers that it *is* signed. But Bowers warns that

> A formula of this sort is seldom used. Because of the reversal of the order of details within the parentheses, quoting of the interpolation must always be adopted to avoid ambiguity [with the regular signing.] [239 +1.]

§6.10 A–C^4 ***D1** D–E^4.

» *Bowers:* A–C^4 ***D1** D–E^4.
The insertion is not associated with the succeeding gathering.

» *Alternative:* A–C^4 D^4(***D1+D1**) E^4.
Quoting the insertion is not necessary, because its signing is unique, but doing so may add to clarity.

B. *Separate (disjunct) leaves inside the gathering.*

¶ Separate leaves inside the gathering must be associated with the preceding leaf of the regular signing, in order to indicate their position within the gathering. This type of insertion is indicated in the same manner as insertion outside the gathering (a plus sign followed by the signature of the insertion).

Some examples:

§6.11 A–B^4 [C1 C2 C3 **C4** C4] D^4.

A leaf signed **C4** is inserted between the regular **C3** and **C4** leaves.

» *Bowers:* A–B^4 C^4(**C3+‘C4’**) D^4.
The insertion signed **C4** must be quoted because it duplicates the regular **C4** signing. Quoting informs readers that the insertion *is* signed.

» *Tanselle:* A–B^4 C^4(**C3+1**) D^4.
Tanselle states that

Insertions are subordinate to the gatherings of which they have become a part, and their signatures thus have a different standing from the signatures of the primary gatherings. [72 +4.]

The actual signing of the insertion (replaced by the positional indicator **+1**) is reported in the statement of signing: **C3(1)** = **C4**. The meaning of this statement is: the single leaf inserted after **C3** is signed **C4**.

§6.12 A–B^4 [C1 C2 C3 **4** C4] D^4.

The insertion bears only the direction number **4**.

» *Bowers:* A–B^4 C^4(**C3+'4'**) D^4.
The need to quote the insertion is very strong because its signing, just a direction-number, is anomalous. Quotes also obviate the suggestion that **4** may mean 4 disjunct leaves.

» *Conservative approach:* A–B^4 C^4(**C3+χ1**) D^4.
The direction number of the insertion is ignored, and the leaf is treated as if unsigned (**χ1**), but its signing is noted in the statement of signing: **C(χ1)** signed **'4'**.

» *Tanselle:* A–B^4 C^4(**C3+1**) D^4.
The direction number of the insertion (replaced by the positional indicator **+1**) is reported in the statement of signing: **C3(1)** = **4**. The meaning of this statement is: the single leaf inserted after **C3** is direction-numbered '**4**'.

§6.13 A–B^4 [C1 C2 C3 **[unsigned leaf]** C4] D^4.

An unsigned leaf is inserted between leaves **C3** and **C4**.

» *Bowers (preferred):* A–B^4 C^4(**C3+χ1**) D^4.
The insertion is unsigned and uninferrable: there is no peg on which to hang the inference.

» *Bowers (alternative):* A–B^4 C^4(**C3+1**) D^4.
Bowers's positional solution.

» *Tanselle:* A–B^4 C^4(**C3+1**) D^4.
Rejection of the use of the symbol χ for insertions in favour of the positional notation **+1**.

§6.14 A–B^4 [C1 C2 C3 **C4** **[unsigned leaf]** C4] D^4.

A leaf signed **C4** is inserted after the regular **C3** leaf and is followed by an unsigned leaf. This type of insertion presents problems of inference.

» *Bowers (preferred):* A–B^4 C^4(**C3+'C4',χ1**) D^4.

The insertion signed **C4** must be quoted to distinguish it from the regular **C4** signing. The unsigned insertion cannot be inferred as **C5** because, although this signing would be unique, it would also be very confusing: a **C5** leaf appearing before the regular **C4** leaf. Bowers's position is that

> For these disjunct leaves within a gathering the safest practice is not to infer signings unless one is forced to. [239 -14.]

In other words, this is a

> Refusal to perpetuate inferentially an anomalous signing. [246 -3.]

The signed insertion **C4** *is* an anomalous signing (it duplicates the regular **C4** signing); therefore, the unsigned leaf cannot be inferred as **C5**.

N.B. Compare this with *Example §6.7* where the unsigned inserted leaves had their signings inferred because of their 'ultimate and unambiguous' position.

» *Bowers (alternative):* A–B^4 C^4(**C3+'C4'+1**) D^4.
Bowers's positional solution.

» *Tanselle:* A–B^4 C^4(**C3+1,2**) D^4.
Rejection of the use of the symbol χ for insertions in favour of the positional notation **+1,2**. The actual signing of the first insertion (replaced by the positional indicator **+1**) is reported in the statement of signing: **C3(1) = C4.**

N.B. Tanselle seems to prefer the notation **+1,2** to the **+2** alternative.

§6.15 A–B^4 [C1 C2 C3 **c2** **[unsigned leaf]** C4] D^4.

The first insertion is a leaf signed with a lower-case **c**. Again, this raises problems of inference.

» *Bowers (preferred):* A–B^4 C^4(**C3+c2,χ1**) D^4.
Quoting the insertion is not necessary because its signing is unique (it is in lower case). It would be possible to infer the unsigned insertion as **c3** because this signing would also be unique, but Bowers discourages this approach, as **c2** is an anomalous signing; again, his

> Refusal to perpetuate inferentially an anomalous signing. [246 -3.]

» *Bowers (alternative):* A–B^4 C^4(**C3+c2+1**) D^4.
Bowers's positional solution.

» *Alternative (inference):* A–B^4 C^4(**C3+'c2',c3**) D^4.

The signed insertion must be quoted to make it clear that it is signed, and to indicate that **c3**, not in quotes, is an inference.

» *Tanselle:* A–B^4 C^4(**C3+1,2**) D^4.
Rejection of the use of the symbol χ for insertions in favour of the positional notation **+1,2**. The actual signing of the first insertion (replaced by the positional indicator **+1**) is reported in the statement of signing: **C3(1) = c2**.

C. *Miscellaneous notes.*

¶ The symbol χ *inside parentheses* is never doubled:

» A–B^4 **χ1** C^4 D^4(D4+D5) E^4(E3+**χ1**) *not* E^4(E3+**2χ1**).
In other words, the χ symbol employed for the insertion cannot be counted as the second in the collation. The reference to the first χ leaf is **χ1**, whereas the reference to the second χ leaf is **E(χ1)**: there is no possibility of confusion.

¶ The dash is never used with insertions or deletions:

» C^4(C4+**'C5',C6,C7**) *not* C^4(C4+'C5',**C6–7**).

The shorthand notation **C6–7** cannot be used because it does not make clear whether the leaves are conjugate or disjunct.

¶ It is *not* customary to associate a *final* unsigned leaf with the preceding gathering:

» A–P^4 **χ1** *or* A–P^4 **[Q]1** *not* A–O^4 P^4(**P4+χ1**) *or* A–O^4 P^4(**P4+1**).

D. *Folds outside the gathering.*

(a) Folds, either unsigned or signed on the first leaf with a presumed '1'.

¶ According to Bowers

> Signed or unsigned folds inserted between gatherings are treated as separate gatherings if the signature of their first leaf begins with a presumed '1'. [241 +5]

and

> They are necessarily treated in the formula as separate items because they were signed and numbered by the printer as separate gatherings. [241 +15.]

Again, Bowers's insistence on following printer's intentions. There seems to be a universal agreement on this point. Some examples follow (the full stop between leaves is the usual shorthand for conjugacy).

§6.16 A–D^4 2D^2 E–2G^4.

» *Bowers:* A–D^4 $^{\chi}$**2D^2** E–2G^4.
Here we have two gatherings signed **2D**, the first is an insertion placed after gathering **D**, whereas the second appears within the doubled signings **2A–2G**. The symbol χ must be added to the signing of the insertion as a prefixed index. There are no alternatives to this approach.

§6.17 A–C^4 D^4 ***D.*D2.[unsigned leaf].[unsigned leaf]** E^4.

A 4-leaf gathering with the first two leaves respectively signed ***D** (with a *presumed 1*) and ***D2**, and the last two leaves unsigned, is inserted after the regular signature **D**:

» A–D^4 ***D^4** E^4 *not* A–C^4 D^4(**D^4+*D^4**) E^4.
There are no alternatives to this approach.

> **N.B.** Signature ***D** is unique and does not duplicate any other signature, therefore there is no need to prefix it with the χ index.

§6.18 A–C^4 D^4 [unsigned leaf].[unsigned leaf].[unsigned leaf].[unsigned leaf] E^4.

A 4-leaf unsigned gathering is inserted between gatherings **D** and **E**:

» A–D^4 χ^4 E^4.
No inference is possible for the unsigned gatherings and the symbol χ must therefore be used. There are no alternatives to this approach.

(b) Signed folds continuing or duplicating the numbering of a preceding gathering.

Here there *are* differences of opinion, Bowers preferring association and a freer inference:

> In folds or gatherings the signing is ordinarily established by the first leaf. Hence when there is no conflict with the signing and numbering of the leaves of the regular gathering, there is less need than with disjunct leaves to be precise in marking the inferred signing of unsigned conjugate leaves. [242 +7.]

Some examples follow.

§6.19 A–C^{4} D^{4} *D4.[unsigned leaf].[unsigned leaf].[unsigned leaf] E^{4}.

A 4-leaf gathering with the first leaf signed ***D4** and the other leaves unsigned, is inserted after the regular signature **D**:

» *Bowers:* A–C^{4} D^{4}(**D4+*D4.5.6.7**) E^{4}.

The first leaf of the inserted gathering, although signed with an asterisk (*), is direction-numbered **4**, and therefore the inserted gathering needs to be associated with the regular **D** gathering. The shorthand notation employed to indicate conjugacy of consecutive leaves, ***D4.5.6.7**, means: ***D4** is conjugate with ***D7**, ***D5** with ***D6**. The signature ***D4** does not need to be quoted because it does not conflict with any regular signing.

Had this been the case of an insertion of disjunct leaves, leaf ***D4** would have been quoted and the following three leaves would have been understood to be unsigned: **'*D4',D5,D6,D7** (*Example §6.7*). But, in this case, ***D4** is without quotes, and it is not made explicit whether the following three leaves are signed or not.

» *No association:* A–D^{4} ^{x}**D^{4}** E^{4}.

Fold ***D4** is not associated to gathering **D** but is treated in the collation as a separate element. The actual signing of the insertion is reported in the statement of signing: ^{x}**D1** signed ***D4**.

§6.20 A–C^{4} D^{4} D4.[unsigned leaf].[unsigned leaf].[unsigned leaf] E^{4}.

A four-leaf gathering, with the first leaf signed **D4** and the other leaves unsigned, is inserted after the regular signature **D**.

» *Bowers:* A–C^{4} D^{4}(**D4+'D4'.5.6.7**) E^{4}.

The first leaf of the inserted gathering is signed **D4**, and therefore the gathering needs to be associated with the regular **D** gathering. The insertion **D4** is quoted to distinguish it from the regular **D4** signing, and to inform readers that it is signed, whereas the three insertions immediately following it are inferred.

» *No association:* A–D^{4} ^{x}**D^{4}** E^{4}.

The inserted fold is not associated with gathering **D** but is treated in the collation as a separate element. The actual signing of the insertion is reported in the statement of signing: ^{x}**D1** signed ***D4**.

§6.21 A–D^{4} *D5 *D6.[unsigned leaf] E^{4}.

After **D4** comes a leaf signed ***D5** and a bifolium with the first leaf signed ***D6**.

» *Bowers:* A–C^4 D^4(**D4+*D5,*D6.7**) E^4.
The first two leaves of the inserted gathering, although signed with an asterisk (*), are direction-numbered **5** and **6**, and therefore need to be associated with the regular **D** gathering. The insertions ***D5** and ***D6** do not need to be quoted because they do not conflict with any regular signing. The leaf conjugate with ***D6** is inferred as ***D7** but, unlike the previous example, the collation does not make it clear whether this leaf conjugate with ***D6** is signed or not.

» *No association:* A–D^4 ***D1** ^{x*}**D**^{2} E^4.
The inserted leaf and fold are not associated to gatherings **D** and are treated in the collation as separate elements. The actual signings of the insertions are reported in the statement of signing: ***D1** signed ***D5**, ^{x*}**D1** signed ***D6**.

E. *Folds inside the gathering.*

Folds inside the gathering must be associated with the preceding leaf. The question is whether or not to infer inserted unsigned leaves which are conjugate with a signed one when they would conflict with regular signings.

Whereas Tanselle's method is purely positional in the notation of all types of inserts, and therefore extremely clear and logic (see the *Introduction* to this section), Bowers's method is a little ambiguous in its treatment of inserted folds. Let us consider three examples.

» E^4(E1+**E2.1**).
The notation **.1** is obviously not an inferred signing i.e., leaf **E1**, but simply tells us that an unsigned leaf is conjugate with signed leaf **E2**.

» D4(D4+***D4.5.6.7**).
Here, *on the contrary*, the notation **.5.6.7** means that the three leaves in the fold following signed leaf ***D4** have been inferred as ***D5**, ***D6** and ***D7**.

» D4(D2+***d1.2**).
In this case all we can be sure of is that the first leaf is signed **d** (with a presumed 1). What the notation **.2** used for its conjugate leaf stand for is less clear. It could either suggest the inference of the second leaf as ***d2** or it could mean '*second* leaf in the fold, conjugate with **d1**'. I presume that Bowers intends the inference of the second leaf as ***d2**.

(a) Folds signed on the first leaf with a number other than '1'.

In cases such as these Bowers discourages inference, even when the signature of the insertion is different from that of the normal gathering, as in this case: **d** instead of **D**. Again, Bowers's

> Refusal to perpetuate inferentially an anomalous signing. [246 -3.]

A few examples:

§6.22 A–D^4 [E1 E2.[unsigned leaf] E2 E3 E4] F^4.

A bifolium, with the first leaf signed **E2** and its conjugate leaf unsigned, is inserted after leaf **E1**.

» *Bowers:* A–D^4 E^4(**E1+'E2'.1**) F^4.

The inserted leaf **E2** must be quoted in order to differentiate it from the regular **E2** signing. To infer the conjugate unsigned leaf as **E3** would create confusion, as it would duplicate the regular **E3** signing, hence the preference for the **.1** notation, where the number **1** indicates the unsigned leaf about which no inference as to signing is being made.

> **N.B.** Because the unsigned leaf following **E1** is conjugate with it, they belong to the *same signing*. The unsigned conjugate leaf, therefore, cannot be called χ, because χ is a *different signing*. In other words, we cannot write: E^4(E1+'E2'.χ1). This type of notation is possible only when dealing with unsigned disjunct leaves: E^4(E1+'E2',**χ1**).

» *Tanselle:* A–D^4 E^4(**E1+1.2**) F^4.

The actual signing of the first inserted leaf (replaced by the positional indicator +1) is reported in the statement of signing: **E1(1) = E2**.

§6.23 A–C^4 [D1 D2 D3 **d3.[unsigned leaf]** D4] E–F^4.

A bifolium, with the first leaf signed **d3** and its conjugate leaf unsigned, is inserted after leaf **D3**.

» *Bowers:* A–C^4 D^4(**D3+d3.1**) E–F^4.

Bowers discourages inference, even if the signature of the insertion is different from that of the normal gathering, as in this case (**d** instead of **D**).

Leaf **d3** does not need quoting because its signing is unique.

» *Tanselle:* A–C^4 D^4(**D3+1.2**) E–F^4.

The actual signing of the first leaf of the insertion (replaced by the positional indicator +1) is reported in the statement of signing:
D3(1) = d3.

(b) Folds signed on the first leaf with a presumed '1'.

A few examples follow.

§6.24 A–C^4 [D1 *D.[unsigned leaf] D2 D3 D4] E–F^4.

A bifolium, with the first leaf signed ***D** and its conjugate leaf unsigned, is inserted after leaf **D1**.

In cases such as this Bowers allows two alternative notations: ***D^2** or ***D1.2**:

> So long as it is understood that N^4(N2+n^2) could not be written unless the inserted fold were signed n1 on its first leaf, and so long as the insertions have a differentiating mark from the signing of the original gathering, there would seem sufficient clarity in the shorter form [instead of N^4(N2+n1.2]. [243 +17.]

» *Bowers (preferred):* A–C^4 D^4(**D1+*D^2**) E–F^4.
The signature of the insertion does not need to be quoted, because it does not duplicate any regular signing, being prefixed by an asterisk (*). The notation ***D^2** is allowed because the first leaf of the inserted fold is signed with a presumed **1**.

» *Bowers (alternative):* A–C^4 D^4(**D1+*D1.2**) E–F^4.
The notation ***D^2** can also be expressed as ***D1.2**.

» *Tanselle:* A–C^4 D^4(**D1+1.2**) E–F^4.
The actual signature of the first insertion (replaced by the positional indicator **+1**) is reported in the statement of signing: **D1(1)** = ***D**.

§6.25 A–C^4 [D1 D2 [unsigned leaf].[unsigned leaf] D3 D4] E–F^4.

An unsigned fold is inserted after leaf **D2**.

» *Bowers:* A–C^4 D^4(**D2+χ^2**) E–F^4.
For the unsigned fold the symbol χ must be used, as no inference is possible.

> **N.B.** Bowers does not mention an alternative positional solution—([**signature**]+**1.2**)—for unsigned folds [243 +1], hence I assume he rejects it.

» *Alternative:* A–C^4 **D^6** E–F^4.
Because the insertion is not signed, gathering D in fact consists of six leaves of normal conjugacy. If there is something peculiar about the innermost fold it will be the subject of a note.

» *Tanselle:* A–C^4 D^4(**D2+1.2**) E–F^4.
Rejection of the use of the symbol χ for insertions in favour of the positional notation **+1.2**.

F. *Miscellaneous notes.*

As we have seen, the full-stop, as in **B4.5**, is a sign of conjugacy, and full stops can also be used in a consecutive series. For example, the insertion in quire **D** of a 4-leaf quire with the first two leaves respectively signed ***D4** and ***D5**, can be expressed as D(D4+***D4.5.6.7**). This is a useful convention, even if the conjugacy is properly ***D4.7** and ***D5.6**. Similarly, Brian McMullin suggests that we can extend this convention to an insert of an odd number of leaves, where the one disjunct leaf is found in the middle. For example, we can use the notation D^4(D4+***D4.5.6**) for an insert made up of an unsigned leaf quired in the middle of a fold, the first leaf of which is signed ***D4**. In other words, when a string of numbers joined by full stops (indicating conjugacy) is uneven, it is understood that *the central one is disjunct.*[12] Tanselle, in his reply to McMullin,[13] rejected this proposal preferring, in my opinion, a clumsier D^4(D4+***D1.5, 2.4, 3**).

G. *Reference Notation.*

There are two schools of thought for referencing insertions, Bowers's and Tanselle's.

(a) Bowers's system of reference.

There are three main points to bear in mind when dealing with Bowers's method.

1. ***References can be either condensed or explicit.***

   Condensed references do not make immediately apparent the position of the referenced leaf in the gathering. For example, in G^4(G2+**χ1**) the *condensed* reference to the insert is simply

   » G(χ1).

   An *explicit* reference, on the other hand, is precise about the whereabouts of the referenced leaf in the gathering. The insert of the example above can be referenced as:

[12] B.J. McMullin, 'Bowers's *Principles of Bibliographical Description*,' *Bibliographical Society of Australia and New Zealand Bulletin*, 15 (1991), 53–59 (p. 58).

[13] G. Thomas Tanselle, 'Bowers's *Principles*: Supplementary Notes on Issue, Format, and Insertions,' *Bibliographical Society of Australia and New Zealand Bulletin*, 23 (1999), 107–09 (p. 108).

» G(G2+χ1)
» G2+χ1
» G2+1(χ1)

It is now clear that the insert is to be found immediately after leaf **G2**.

N.B. None of the above references are purely positional because they all require the actual signing, or lack of it (i.e., χ1), of the insert. Furthermore, it is not always possible to construct *condensed* references.

2. ***References to inserts need to be constructed using an* anchor leaf.**

For example, in F⁴(F3+**'F4',χ1**), the reference notations for the *signed* insert are:

» F(F3+'F4')
» F3+'F4'
» F3+1('F4')

where leaf **F3** is the *anchor leaf*. The reference notations for the *unsigned* insert are:

» F(F3+2)
» F3+2
» F('F4'+1).

In cases such as these, choosing a regular signing as *anchor leaf* makes the notation reference clearer, especially when the collation statement is not immediately available to the reader. In F(F3+**2**) the position of the regular leaf **F3** is clear, and all is required is to turn to signature **F3** and count forward two leaves, whereas the reference F('F4'+**1**) requires prior analysis of the position of leaf **'F4'**.

3. ***References to insertions are positional in nature.***

Bowers states that

> The only point in reference is to direct the reader to the precise position of a specific leaf in the gathering. [261 –17.]

So, the reference notations for the second insert in F⁴(F3+'F4',**χ1**) and F4(F3+'F4'.1) are the same:

» F(F3+2).
» F('F4'+**1**).

In other words, in reference (but not in the collation) the notation does not indicate conjugacy.

In reality, Bowers's system still partially relies on the actual signings of the inserts; in fact, the second reference notation above makes use of the signature of the first insert leaf, even retaining the quotation marks:

> Quotation marks in the formula are best preserved in reference since they indicate something unusual. [260 –20.]

The only *truly* positional notation is F(F3+**2**).

(b) Tanselle's system of reference.

Tanselle's system of reference is based on his structural collational system

> With notation that consistently focuses on position, not signing. [77 +13.]

Commenting on Bowers's method of referencing Tanselle maintains that in G(G2+χ1) the first G is repetitious and that in G2+χ1.

> The use of a plus sign that does not fall within parentheses awkwardly makes the notation look like the reference to two entities. [77 +3.]

According to Tanselle's method, Bowers's F^4(F3+**'F4'.1**) and G^4(G2+**χ1**) translate into F^4(F3+**1.2**) and G^4(G2+**1**).

Tanselle's references can therefore all be of the condensed type:

- » F3(1)
- » F3(2)
- » G2(1).

(c) Examples of references.

In the following table only segments of collations are given, and references apply to the elements in **bold**.

Collation segments dealt with according to Bowers's method are prefixed by **(B)**, and their equivalent in Tanselle's method by **(T)**.

Collation segment	Bowers (Explicit reference)	Bowers (Condensed ref)	Tanselle
(B) C4(C2+***C2**)	C(C2+*C2)	C(*C2)	
	C2+*C2		
	C2+1(*C2)		
(T) C4(C2+**1**)			C2(1)
(B) E4(E1+**e1**)	E(E1+e1)	E(e1)	
	E1+e1		
	E1+1(e1)		
(T) E4(E1+**1**)			E1(1)
(B) G4(G2+**χ1**)	G(G2+χ1)	G(χ1)	
	G2+χ1		
	G2+1(χ1)		
(B) G4(G2+**1**)	G(G2+1)		
	G2+1		
(T) G^4(G2+**1**)			G2(1)
(B) K^4(K3+**‘K4’**,χ1)	K(K3+‘K4’)	K(‘K4’)	
	K3+‘K4’		
	K3+1('K4')		
(B) K^4(K3+‘K4’,**χ1**)	K(K3+2)	K(χ1)	
	K3+2		
	K(‘K4’+1)		
	K3+2(χ1)		

Collation segment	Bowers (Explicit reference)	Bowers (Condensed ref)	Tanselle
(B) K^4(K3+‘K4’**+1**)	K(K3+2)	n/a	
	K3+2		
	K(‘K4’+1)		
(T) K^4(K3+**1**,2)			K3(1)
(T) K^4(K3+1,**2**)			K3(2)
(B) A^4(A2+***A^2**)	A(A2+*A1)	A(*A1)	
	A2+*A1		
	A2+1(*A1)		
	A(A2+*A2)	A(*A2)	
	A2+*A2		
	A2+2(*A2)		
N.B. The notations A(A2+*A1) ; A(A2+*A2), and A2+*A1 ; A2+*A2 are ambiguous because could refer to a single leaf insert as in A4(A2+*A1) or A4(A2+*A2)			
(T) A^4(A2+**1**.2)			A2(1)
(T) A^4(A2+1.**2**)			A2(2)
(B) E^4(E3+**e4**.1)	E(E3+e4)	E(e4)	
	E3+e4		
	E3+1(e4)		
(B) E^4(E3+e4.**1**)	E(E3+2)		
	E3+2		
	E(e4+1)		
(T) E^4(E3+**1**.2)			E3(1)

Collation segment	Bowers (Explicit reference)	Bowers (Condensed ref)	Tanselle
(T) E^4(E3+1.**2**)			E3(2)
(T) F^4(F3+**1**.2)			F3(1)
(T) F^4(F3+1.**2**)			F3(2)
(B) $L^4(L1+\boldsymbol{\chi}^2)$	L(L1+1)	L(χ1)	L1(1)
	L1+1		
	L1+1(χ1)		
	L(L1+2)	L(χ2)	L1(2)
	L1+2		
	L1+2(χ2)		

Exercise 4

1 A–C^4 [unsigned leaf] D^4 [unsigned leaf] E–F^4 [leaf signed ¶] [leaf signed ¶2] G–P^4 [unsigned leaf].

2 A–B^4 [unsigned leaf] C^4 [unsigned leaf] D^4 [1 leaf signed D5] E^4 [unsigned leaf after E3] F^4 [leaf direction-numbered 4 after F3] G–Y^4.

3 A–C^4 [1 unsigned leaf] D^4 [after D3, two disjunct leaves, the first signed § and the second unsigned] E^4 F^4 [after F4, two disjunct leaves signed F5 and F6 followed by an unsigned leaf] G–Y^4.

4 A–C^4 D^4 [after D4, one leaf signed ¶5] E^4.

5	[unsigned leaf] B^4 [leaf signed *C] C–G^4 [leaf signed H] H^4 I–M^4.
6	A–D^4 E^4 [after E1, one leaf signed e2; after E3, one leaf signed e4] F–L^4.
7	A–B^4 [C1 C2 ¶.[unsigned leaf] C3 C4] D^4 [E1 E2 E3 e3.[unsigned leaf] E4] F–Y^4
8	A–B^4 [C1 C2 C3 C4.[unsigned leaf] C4] D^4 [E1 E2 E3 [unsigned leaf].[unsigned leaf] E4] F–Y^4

Exercise 4 : Key

1 *Bowers (preferred):* A–C^{4} χ1 D^{4} 2χ1 E–F^{4} ¶1,2 G–P^{4} 3χ1.
Bowers (alternative): A–B4 C^{4}(C4+χ1) D^{4}(D4+χ1) E–F4 ¶1,2 G–P4 χ1.
Bowers (alternative): A–B^{4} C^{4}(C4+1) D^{4}(D4+1) E–F^{4} ¶1,2 *G–P*^{4} χ1.
In all the examples above, if the last leaf continues the text, it can be inferred as [Q]1.

2 *Bowers (preferred):* A–B^{4} χ1 C^{4} 2χ1 D^{4}(D4+D5) E^{4}(E3+χ1) F^{4}(F3+'4') G–Y^{4}.
D5 is signed, but there is no need to quote it (some writers would quote it for the sake of clarity).

The symbol χ inside parentheses is not duplicated: *not* E4(E3+3χ1).

'4' must be quoted because it is an anomalous signing (just a direction-number).

Bowers (alternative): A^{4} B^{4}(B4+χ1) C^{4}(C4+χ1) D^{4}(D4+D5) E^{4}(E3+χ1) F^{4}(F3+'4') G–Y^{4}.

Bowers (alternative): A^{4} B^{4}(B4+1) C^{4}(C4+1) D^{4}(D4+D5) E^{4}(E3+χ1) F^{4}(F3+'4') G–Y^{4}.

No association: A–B^{4} χ1 C^{4} 2χ1 D^{4} $^{\chi}$D1 E^{4}(E3+χ1) F^{4}(F3+'4') G–Y^{4}.

3 *Bowers (preferred):* A–C^{4} χ1 D^{4}(D3+§1,χ1) E^{4} F^{4}(F4+'F5','F6', F7) G–Y^{4}.
Bowers (alternative): A–B^{4} C^{4}(C4+χ1) D^{4}(D3+§1+χ1) E^{4} F^{4}(F4+'F5', 'F6',F7) G–Y^{4}.

Bowers (alternative): A–B^{4} C^{4}(C4+1) D^{4}(D3+§1+χ1) E^{4} F^{4}(F4+'F5', 'F6',F7) G–Y^{4}.

No association: A–C^{4} χ1 D^{4}(D3+§1+1) E–F^{4} χF1,2 2χ1 G–Y^{4}.

The actual signings of the insertions are reported in the statement of signing.

Tanselle: A–C^{4} χ1 D^{4}(D3+1,2) E^{4} F^{4}(F4+1,2,3) G–Y^{4}.

The actual signings of the insertions are reported in the statement of signing.

4 *Bowers:* A–C^{4} D^{4}(D4+'¶5') E^{4}.
No association: A–D^{4} ¶1 E^{4}.

The actual signing of the insertion is reported in the statement of signing.

5 *Bowers:* [A]1 B^{4} *C1 C–G^{4} $^{\chi}$H1 H–M^{4}.

Alternative: [A]1 B^4 C^4(‘*C1’+C1) D–G^4 H^4(‘H1’+H1) I–M^4.

6 *Bowers:* A–D^4 E^4(E1+e2; E3+e4) F–L^4.
Some writers would quote e2 and e4 for the sake of clarity.
Tanselle: A–D^4 E^4(E1+1; E3+1) F–L^4.

The actual signings of the insertions are noted in the statement of signing.

7 *Bowers (preferred):* A–B^4 C^4(C2+¶^{2}) D^4 E^4(E3+e3.1) F–Y^4.
Bowers (alternative): A–B^4 C^4(C2+¶1.2) D^4 E^4(E3+e3.1) F–Y^4.

Alternative: A–B^4 C^4(C2+¶1.2) D^4 E^4(E3+‘e3’.e4) F–Y^4.

Bowers would reject this solution on the grounds that it would perpetuate inferentially an anomalous signing (e3).

Tanselle: A–B^4 C^4(C2+1.2) D^4 E^4(E3+1.2) F–Y^4.

The actual signing of the insertions are reported in the statement of signing.

8 *Bowers (preferred):* A–B^4 C^4(C3+‘C4’.1) D^4 E^4(E3+χ^2) F–Y^4.
Bowers (alternative): A–B^4 C^4(C3+‘C4’.1) D^4 E^4(E3+χ1.2) F–Y^4.

Tanselle: A–B^4 C^4(C3+1.2) D^4 E^4(E3+1.2) F–Y^4.

The actual signing of the insertion is reported in the statement of signing.

§7 CANCELLATION AND SUBSTITUTION

A. *Cancellanda and Cancellantia.*

Before delving into this subject, it is necessary to introduce two new terms. Very often, after a sheet had been printed, mistakes were spotted and needed to be corrected. The simplest way to achieve this was to print a list of errata. Alternatively, whole leaves, or even whole sheets were cancelled (that is removed and replaced by new material).

The cancellation of a single leaf was achieved by cutting it close to the inner margin and by pasting its replacement onto the resulting stub. The leaf needing cancellation is a *cancellandum* (plural *cancellanda*), the leaf replacing it a *cancellans* (plural *cancellantia*), or simply a *cancel.*

Figure 15 shows two leaves of a book. The leaf on the right is attached to a stub (marked with a white star), on which fragments of printed characters can still be seen (two are circled). This stub is all that remains of the original leaf, which, needing replacing, was excised. The *cancellans*, marked with a white dot, is the replacement leaf pasted onto the stub.

Strictly speaking the term *cancellation* means the *removal* of a leaf or leaves and their *replacement*, either at the same place or elsewhere in the gathering, by the same or a different number of leaves. When removal of a leaf or leaves is not followed by substitution, we ought to use the term *excision.* This occurred, for example, when the printer made use of an available leaf by excising it in order to print something for elsewhere in the book or even in another book.

Bowers uses two binomials in his exposition:

- *cancellation and substitution* as a general umbrella term
- *cancellation and insertion* as a more general term in the text.

Insertion in this context is not the 'simple insertion' discussed in *Section 6*, but the second element of the binomial *cancellation and insertion.* As for the term *excision*, Bowers uses it only in the common sense of 'the removal of a leaf or leaves'. I have retained Bowers's usage.

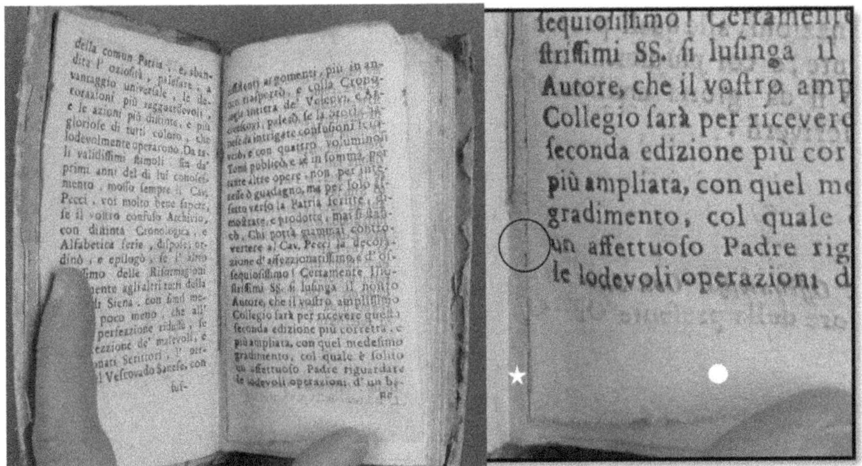

Figure 14: Stub of the cancellandum, and cancellans

B. *Simple cancellation.*

Simple cancellation is indicated by a minus sign. There is no need to quote or infer the signings of cancellanda leaves, as it is impossible to guess their original signatures:

§7.1 A–B^8 [C ~~C2~~ C3 C4 C5 C6 C7 C8].

Leaf C2 has been excised.

» A–B^8 C^8(–**C2**).

§7.2 A–B^8 [C1 ~~C2~~ ~~C3~~ C4 C5 C6 C7 C8].

Disjunct leaves C2 and C3 have been excised.

» A–B^8 C^8(–**C2,3**).

§7.3 A–B^8 [C1 ~~C2~~ C3 C4 C5 C6 ~~C7~~ C8]

Conjugate leaves C2 and C7 have been excised.

» A–B^8 C^8(–**C2.7**).

C. *Cancellation and insertion of equal number of leaves at the same places in the gathering.*

(a) Cancellation followed by insertion expressed with the ± symbol.

Cancellation followed by insertion at the same point in the gathering of:

- equal number of leaves
- same conjugacy
- signed by the same system of signing as that used in the gathering

is indicated by a plus and minus sign (±):

§7.4 A–B^4 [C C2 ~~C3~~ **C3** C4] [D ~~D2~~ **D2** D3 ~~D4~~ **D4**] E–I^4 [K ~~K2~~ **K2** ~~K3~~ **K3** K4] [~~L~~ **L** ~~L2~~ **L2** ~~L3~~ **L3** ~~L4~~ **L4**] =

» A–B^4 C^4(**±C3**) D^4(**±D2,4**) E–I^4 K^4(**±K2.3**) L^4(**±**).
The meaning of the ± notations is:

- cancellandum **C3** has been replaced by cancellans **C3**
- disjunct cancellanda **D2** and **D4** have been replaced by disjunct cancellantia **D2** and **D4**
- conjugate cancellanda **K2** and **K3** have been replaced by conjugate cancellantia **K2** and **K3**
- cancellandum gathering **L** of four leaves has been replaced by a cancellans gathering **L** of four leaves of normal conjugacy.

Bowers encourages a very free inference when the ± symbol is employed, dropping quoting altogether:

> With the simultaneous plus and minus signs it is very awkward to try to indicate the signing or lack of signing of the cancellans. Hence all quoting is dropped. [244 –19.]

In fact, it is clear that a notation such as **C^4(±‘C3’)**, with the cancellans leaf within quotes might mean that *both* cancellandum *and* cancellans were signed **‘C3’**; in other words, at least one copy of the edition is known to retain the cancellandum leaf signed **C3**. But it would be impossible, or extremely awkward, to convey the fact that the cancellandum was not signed but the cancellans is. Therefore, we use the statement of signing instead, to cover the signing of *all* leaves.

b. Cancellation followed by insertion expressed with the plus (+) and minus (–) symbols in an expanded formula.

If cancellation is followed by insertion of:

- equal number of leaves
- different conjugacy (or lack of conjugacy) and/or
- signed by a different system of signing than that used in the gathering

an expanded notation is necessary, beginning with the minus sign. Bowers advocates a liberal use of inference and the application of the principles of simple insertion (*Section 6*). A few examples follow.

§7.5 A–B^4 C^4(–**C3,4 + [unsigned leaf].[unsigned leaf]**) D^4.

We are dealing here with an unsigned cancellation and insertion of:

- same number of leaves
- in the same position
- with different conjugacy (a bifolium replaces two disjunct leaves):

» *Bowers:* A–B^4 C^4(**–C3,4+C3.4**) D^4.
Both cancellantia are unsigned, but they can be inferred as **C3** and **C4** because they *replace* cancellanda **C3** and **C4** in what were their original positions.

» *Conservative approach:* A–B^4 C^4(**–C3,4+χ^2**) D^4.
The signings of the cancellantia are not inferred. The argument for this approach is that both cancellantia are *unsigned*; Bowers's solution would be justified only if the first cancellans were signed **C3**.

» *Tanselle:* A–B^4 C^4(**–C3,4+C3.4**) D^4.
The leaves replacing cancellanda **C3,4** are rendered as **+C3.4** rather than by the positional notation **+1.2** used by Tanselle for simple insertions because *cancellation and substitution* is different from simple *addition*; cancellantia **C3** and **C4** are not *subordinate* to the gathering of which they are part (*Example §6.11*) but are an integral part of it: they *replace* cancelled leaves, they are not just *additions* to the gathering.

§7.6 A–B^4 C^4(–**C4 + [leaf signed c4]**) D^4.

This is a case of cancellation followed by insertion using a different system of signing.

» *Bowers:* A–B^4 C^4(**–C4+c4**) D^4.
We cannot use the ± symbol because **cancellandum C4** belongs to a

gathering signed in upper-case, whereas **cancellans c4** is signed in lower-case.

» *Alternative:* A–B^4 C^4(±**C4**) D^4.

§7.7 A–B^4 C^4(-**C1,2** + **[leaf signed *C].[unsigned leaf]**) D^4.

An instance of cancellation followed by insertion using a different system of signing and different conjugacy.

» *Bowers (preferred):* A–B^4 C^4(–**C1,2**+***C^2**) D^4.
We cannot use the ± symbol because a fold signed ***C** has replaced two disjunct leaves signed **C1** and **C2**. The cancellantia can be expressed as ***C^2** because its first leaf is signed with a presumed **1**.

» *Bowers (alternative):* A–B^4 C^4(–**C1,2**+***C1.2**) D^4.

» *Alternative*: A–B^4 C^4(-**C1,2**+**C1.2**) D^4.
The actual signing of the cancellans is reported in the statement of signing: **C(C1) = *C**.

D. *Cancellation and insertion of different number of leaves starting at the same place in the gathering.*

If cancellation is followed by the insertion at the same point in the gathering of a different number of leaves, an expanded formula is necessary, beginning with the minus sign. The principles governing simple insertion apply (*Section* 6). According to Bowers

> When insertion is greater or less than cancellation, the expanded formula is employed and the treatment of inserts is rather conservative. [249 +3.]

A few examples follow.

§7.8 A^4 B^4 [–**B4** + **[leaf signed B4],[unsigned leaf]**] C^4.

Leaf **B4** has been cancelled and replaced by two disjunct leaves, the first of which is signed **B4**.

» *Bowers (preferred):* A^4 B^4(–**B4**+**'B4',B5**) C^4.
The last inserted leaf can be inferred as **B5** because it does not duplicate any regular signing, **cancellans B4** providing the peg on which to hang the inference, and because of its ultimate and unambiguous position. According to the principles of insertion (*Example* §6.7) the lack of quoting for **B5** means that its signing has been inferred.

N.B. Cancellans B4 is not an anomalous signing, because the original **B4** has been cancelled, making **cancellans B4** the equivalent of the original (unsigned) **B4**. We are *not* perpetuating inferentially an anomalous signing.

» *Bowers (alternative):* A^4 B^4(±**B4+1**) C^4.
If we employ the ± sign, the second insertion needs to be treated positionally and preceded by the plus sign.

The notation **B^4(±B4,1)**, used by some writers, is confusing, because it suggests that *two* leaves have been cancelled and replaced by another two, whereas in fact only *one* leaf has been cancelled and replaced by two leaves. More emphatically a notation such as **B^4(±B4,χ1)** is definitely wrong (in fact incomprehensible) because it implies that a supposed **cancellans B4** and a supposed cancellans χ1 (!) have been replaced by **cancellantia B4** and χ1 (!)

» *Tanselle:* A^4 B^4(±**B4+1**) C^4.
The unsigned insertion is treated positionally (**+1**) and all quoting is dispensed with. The fact that **cancellans B4** is signed is reported in the statement of signing.

In most of the following examples Bowers discourages inference, opting for a conservative approach.

§7.9 A^4 B^4 [**–B3 + [leaf signed B3],[unsigned leaf]**] C^4.

Leaf **B3** has been cancelled and replaced by two disjunct leaves, the first of which is signed **B3**.

» *Bowers (preferred):* A^4 B^4(**–B3+‘B3’,χ1**) C^4.
Cancellans B3 is in quotes because it is signed although quoting is not essential as we are dealing with *cancellation and substitution*, not simple *insertion*. We cannot infer the unsigned insertion as **B4** because that would duplicate the regular **B4** signing.

» *Bowers (alternative):* A^4 B^4(±**B3+1**) C^4.
If we employ the ± sign, the second insertion needs to be treated positionally and preceded by the plus sign. The fact that **cancellans B3** is signed is noted in the statement of signing.

» *Tanselle:* A^4 B^4(±**B3+1**) C^4.
The unsigned insertion is treated positionally (**+1**) and all quoting is dispensed with. The fact that **cancellans B3** is signed is reported in the statement of signing.

§7.10 A^4 B^4 [–B3 + [leaf signed B3].[unsigned leaf]] C^4.

Leaf **B3** has been cancelled and replaced by a bifolium, the first leaf of which is signed **B3**.

» *Bowers:* A^4 B^4(**–B3+'B3'.1**) C^4.
Cancellans B3 is in quotes because it is signed although quoting is not essential as we are dealing with *cancellation and substitution*, not simple *insertion*. The unsigned insertion cannot be inferred as **B4** because that would duplicate the regular **B4** signing. The ± technique cannot be employed because **cancellandum B3** has been replaced by a *bifolium* (two conjugate leaves).

> **NB:** A notation such as B^4(**±B3.1**) is wrong because it implies that supposed **cancellanda B3.1** have been replaced by **cancellantia B3.1**. The unsigned leaf cannot be denoted by the symbol **χ** i.e., B^4(**±B3. χ1**), because it is conjugate with leaf **B3**: it is not an independent signing.

» *Tanselle:* A^4 B^4(**–B3+1.2**) C^4.
The cancellans bifolium is treated positionally (**+1.2**) and the signing of its first leaf is reported in the statement of signing.

§7.11 A^4 B^4 [–B3 + [unsigned leaf].[unsigned leaf]] C^4.

Leaf **B3** has been cancelled and replaced by an unsigned bifolium.

» *Bowers:* A^4 B^4(**–B3+χ^2**) C^4.
We cannot infer either of the two unsigned leaves because there is no peg on which to hang the inference. Inferring the first leaf of the cancellans bifolium as **B4** would duplicate the normal **B4** signing.

» *Bowers (alternative):* A^4 B^4(**–B3+1.2**) C^4.
The cancellans fold is treated positionally (**+1.2**).

» *Tanselle:* A^4 B^4(**–B3+1.2**) C^4.
The cancellans fold is treated positionally (**+1.2**).

§7.12 A^4 B^4 [–B1 + [leaf signed B].[unsigned leaf]] C^4.

Leaf **B1** has been cancelled and replaced by a bifolium the first leaf of which is signed **B**.

» *Bowers (preferred):* A^4 B^4(**–B1+B^2**) C^4.
The ± sign cannot be employed because **cancellandum B1** has been replaced by a *bifolium*. We *can* use the notation **B^2** because the first leaf of this fold is signed with a presumed **1**. It is not made explicit whether the leaf conjugate with **cancellans B1** is signed or not.

» *Bowers (alternative):* A⁴ B⁴(**–B1+B1.2**) C⁴.
It is not necessary to quote **'B1'** because this leaf has the same signing of the leaf which it replaces.

» *Tanselle:* A⁴ B⁴(**–B1+1.2**) C⁴.
The cancellans fold is treated positionally (**+1.2**) and the signing of its first leaf is reported in the statement of signing.

E. *Cancellation and insertion occurring at different places in a gathering.*

When cancellation and insertion occur at different places in the same gathering an expanded formula is necessary. The principles of simple insertion apply (*Section* 6). Bowers prefers to start the collation with the plus sign (+), whereas other writers prefer to start with the minus sign (–):

> Insertion and cancellation may occur at different places in the same gathering, in which case it is clearer to treat the insertion first. [249 –4.]

§7.13 A⁴ [B1 ~~**B2**~~ B3 **[leaf signed B4]** B4] C⁴.

Leaf **B2** has been excised and not replaced, and a leaf signed **B4** has been inserted between **B3** and **B4**.

» *Bowers:* A⁴ B⁴(**B3+'B4'; –B2**) C⁴.
The signing of the insert needs to be quoted because it duplicates the regular **B4** signing.

» *Alternative:* A⁴ B⁴(**–B2; B3+'B4'**) C⁴.

» *Tanselle:* A⁴ B⁴(**B3+1; –B2**) C⁴.
The cancellans leaf is treated positionally (**+1**) and its signing is recorded in the statement of signing.

The usual alternative approaches discussed in *Section* 6 also apply here.

F. *Reference notation.*

When there is cancellation and substitution of leaves, apart from the usual need to uniquely identify each leaf, we also ought to be able to differentiate between the cancellandum (which may survive in some copies) and the cancellans (which may be lacking in some).

Collation segment	Bowers (Explicit reference)	Bowers (Condensed reference)	Tanselle
C^{4}(±**C3**)	cancellandum C3	C3	C3
	cancellans C3	C(C3)	C3(±)
C^{4}(±**C2.3**) *and* C^{4}(–**C2.3** +**C2,3**)	cancellandum C2	C2	C2
	cancellandum C3	C3	C3
	cancellans C2	C(C2)	C2(±)
	cancellans C3	C(C3)	C3(±)
In the examples listed below references for cancellanda are not given, as they follow the pattern of the examples above.			
C^{4}(–C4+**c4**)	Cancellans c4	C(c4)	
C^{4}(–C1,2+***C**^{2})	Cancellans *C1	C(*C1)	
	Cancellans *C2	C(*C2)	
B^{4}(–B3+**B3**,χ1)	Cancellans B3	B(B3)	
B^{4}(–B3+B3,**χ1**)		B(χ1)	
	B(B3+χ1)		
B^{8}(–B7+**χ**^{2})	1st cancellans leaf: B(B6+1)	1st cancellans leaf: B(χ1)	
	2nd cancellans leaf: B(B6+2)	2nd cancellans leaf: B(χ2)	

Collation segment	Bowers (Explicit reference)	Bowers (Condensed reference)	Tanselle
B^4(–B1+**1**.2)			B1(1)
B^4(–B1+1.**2**)			B1(2)

Exercise 5

1	A–B^4
	C^4 (C3 replaced by a leaf signed C3)
	D^4 (D2 replaced by a leaf signed D2, and D4 replaced by an unsigned leaf)
	E–I^4
	K^4 (conjugate K2 and K3 replaced by a fold with its first leaf signed K2 and its second unsigned)
	L^4 (replaced by a complete cancellans gathering L^4).
2	A–L^4
	M^4 (disjunct M1,2 replaced by a bifolium with its first leaf signed M1 and its second unsigned)
	N^4 (fold N2.3 replaced by two disjunct leaves signed N2 and N3)
	O^4 (disjunct unsigned O3,4 replaced by an unsigned bifolium)
	P^4.

3	A^4 (A1 replaced by an unsigned bifolium) B–D^4
	E^4 (E3 replaced by a leaf signed E3 followed by an unsigned disjunct leaf) F–Y^4.
4	a^4 (a1 replaced by an unsigned bifolium) A–F^4
	G^4 (G4 replaced by two disjunct leaves, the first signed G4 and the second unsigned) H^4.

Exercise 5 : Key

1 A–B^4 C^4(±C3) D^4(±D2,4) E–I^4 K^4(±K2.3) L^4(±).
No quoting or inference is necessary.

2 *Bowers preferred:* A–L^4 M^4(–M1,2+M^2) N^4(–N2.3+N2,3) O^4(–O3,4+O3.4) p^4 *or*
M^4(–M1,2+M1.2).

Conservative approach: A–L^4 M^4(–M1,2+M^2) N^4(–N2.3+N2,3) O^4(–O3,4+χ^2) P^4.

Tanselle: A–L^4 M^4(–M1,2+1.2) N^4(–N2.3+1,2) O^4(–O3,4+1.2) P^4.

3 *Bowers (preferred):* A^4(–A1+χ^2) B–D^4 E^4(–E3+E3,χ1) F–Y^4.
Gathering A is the first gathering of the main alphabetical series; it is not a *prefixed* gathering and for this reason the symbol for the unsigned fold must be χ, not π. No inference is possible for the second insertion.

Bowers (alternative): A^4(–A1+χ^2) B–D^4 E^4(±E3+χ1) F–Y^4.

Bowers (alternative): A^4(–A1+χ^2) B–D^4 E^4(±E3+1) F–Y^4.

Tanselle: A^4(–A1+1.2) B–D^4 E^4(±E3+1) F–Y^4.

4 *Bowers (preferred):* a^4(–a1+π^2) A–F^4 G^4(–G4+‘G4’,G5) H^4.
Gathering a is a *prefixed* gathering, therefore the symbol for the unsigned fold must be π. The unsigned insertion in gathering G is inferred as G5 (the lack of quotation marks points to the fact that the leaf is unsigned). ‘G4’ provides the peg on which to hang the inference.

Bowers (alternative): a^4(–a1+π^2) A–F^4 G^4(–G4+‘G4’,χ1) H^4.

Bowers (alternative): a^4(–a1+π^2) A–F^4 G^4(±G4+1) H^4.

Tanselle: a^4(–a1+1.2) A–F^4 G^4(±G4+1) H^4.

§8 STATEMENT OF SIGNING

A. *Definition.*

The statement of signing records which leaves in each gathering are normally signed, any departure from this norm, and a note of misprints. It is generally placed, within brackets, immediately after the collation. Alternatively, it can form a new paragraph.

B. *Bowers vs Tanselle.*

Bowers's method of writing a statement of signing is widely employed, but Tanselle has proposed some useful improvements.

(a) Bowers's method.

Bowers employs, within brackets, the symbol **$** followed by the number of signed leaves and references to any misprints. The symbol **$** is used when we wish to make a statement that applies to 'any signature' or 'every signature'. For example: '**$3** signed' (i.e., in every gathering the first three leaves are signed) or, 'Whenever the text of a quarto ends on **$3**, there is the possibility that **$4** will be used to print a cancellans for the book'.

> **N.B.** As W. W. Greg points out, 'it may, however, be desirable to draw attention to the slightly ambiguous way in which we use the term "signature" to mean either the actual printed signature on a recto page, or the leaf defined by a particular signature, say C2, or the quire defined by a signature letter (or sign), say C or ¶.'[14]

The statement of signing comes soon after the collation. For example:

» A–K^8 [**$4** (–K3; +B5) **signed**; misprinting D2 as D3].

Alternatively, we could write:

» A–K^8 [**$4 signed** (–K3; +B5); misprinting D2 as D3].

The meaning of the above statements is: in each gathering only the first four leaves are signed (**$4**), except in gathering **K**, where leaf **K3** is unsigned,

[14] W. W. Greg, *A Bibliography of the English Printed Drama to the Restoration*, vol. 4, *Introduction* (London: Bibliographical Society, 1959), cliv, n†.

and in gathering **B**, where leaf **B5** too is signed; furthermore, leaf **D2** is misprinted **D3**.

Bowers also allows the retention, in the statement of signing, of all quotation marks present in the collation.

In the example above all gatherings are in 8s and so the statement '$4 signed' covers all gatherings. But a book may be made up of gatherings of different number of leaves: A^{4} $B\text{–}N^{12}$ O^{8} where gathering **A** is signed A1,2, the **B–N** sequence is signed 1–6, and gathering **O** is signed O1–4. Because the majority of gatherings are '$6 signed', we use that as the general statement, refining it with the information that in gathering **A** only two leaves are signed, and that in gathering **O** only four leaves are signed. The statement of signing reads:

» [$6 signed (–A3,4, O5,6)].

This is necessary, otherwise readers may think that leaves **A3,4** and **O5,6** too are signed. This simple technique is made a little more complicated when gatherings are made irregular by insertion and cancellation of leaves. In cases such as these, Bowers states that:

> In gatherings made irregular by interpolations or cancellans leaves, the statement of signing need not take account of these leaves if their signing is quoted in the collational formula; if the signing or lack of signing is not recorded in the collation, the statement covers any necessary notation. [270 -7.]

To sum up, the statement of signing comprises three elements:

- an account of the normal pattern of signed leaves in each gathering
- an account of any deviation from this norm
- an account of any irregular signing.

(b) Tanselle's method.

According to Tanselle a statement such as '$4 signed' strictly speaking means that every fourth leaf of each gathering is signed, and needs the *inference* that, in each gathering, the leaves preceding the designated one are signed too; he advocates the more precise notation **$1–4 signed** or just **$1–4**. The account of any irregular signing will always need to include interpolations or cancellantia, because they are treated positionally and their signing is ignored, Bowers's (C3+'C4',χ1) being expressed as (C3+1,2). *Any leaves not* *mentioned in the statement of signing are assumed unsigned.* The word 'misprinted' is replaced by an equal sign (=). Brackets and the word 'signed' are dispensed with.

Bowers's

» A–B^8 C^8(C3+'C4',χ1) D–M^8. [$4 (–K3; +B5) signed; misprinting D2 as D3]
is rendered as:

» A–B^8 C^8(C3+1,2) D–M^8. *Signatures:* $1–4(–K3; +B5); C3(1)=C4, D2=D3.
Leaf C3(2) is not listed because unsigned.

(c) Interpolations and cancellans leaves.

As already discussed, interpolations and cancellans leaves have special referencing rules. For example, the cancellans in D4(±**D3**) is referenced as **D(D3)** (Bowers) or **D3**(±) (Tanselle) because **D3** is the reference notation for the *cancellandum*. The question is whether these special rules need to be carried out when referencing such leaves in the statement of signing.

Bowers offers only one example [270 –2]:

A–C^4 D^4(±**D3**) E–F^4 G^4(G4+'G5',G6) H^4(H1+***H2**) I^4. [$3 (–**D[D3]**, **H[*H2]**), signed].

It seems, therefore, that he would advocate precise referencing for interpolations and cancellans leaves. Note that Bowers has employed brackets for the reference notations, instead of parentheses; this is to improve legibility, as one would normally write: [$3 (–D(D3), H(*H2)) signed], resulting in two consecutive closing parentheses.

Tanselle is not explicit on this point. However, judging by the examples he provides, he seems to argue that although the exact reference for **cancellans D3** is **D3**(±), in practice the cancellans is the only leaf, of the two, that remains, and may be referenced simply as **D3**. The statement of signing describes the ideal copy and if a copy contains both cancellandum and cancellans, or the cancellandum only, that peculiarity is a matter for a note, not the statement of signing. In other words, it is evident that **D3** can only refer to the cancellans, because there is no other leaf that can be so described.

Similarly, we could write:

A–C^4 D^4(±**D3**) E–F^4 G^4(–G3,4+**G3**.4) H^4. [$3 (–**D3**, **G3**) signed]
instead of [$3 (–**D[D3]**, **G[G3]**) signed].

(d) Bowers vs Tanselle in practice.

To show in practice the difference between the two methods I will compare some collations, one written according to Bowers's method and the other according to Tanselle's (differences in **bold**). Each collation will be followed by its statement of signing.

§8.1 Bowers *and* Tanselle: A–C^4 D^4(**±D4**) E–M^4.

In gathering **D**, leaf **D4** has been cancelled and replaced by another leaf. Because the collation does not make clear whether this cancellans is signed or not, we must make this clear in the statement of signing.

» *Bowers (cancellans* signed*):* [$2(+D[D4]) signed.

» *Bowers (cancellans* not signed*):* [$2 signed].

» *Tanselle (cancellans* signed*): Signatures:* $1–2(+D4).

» *Tanselle (cancellans* not signed*): Signatures:* $1–2.

§8.2 Bowers: A–C^4 D^4(**D4+D5**) E–M^4.

In gathering **D**, a leaf signed **D5** is inserted after **D4**. The collation makes it clear that the insertion **D5** is signed by *not* quoting it (*Example §6.4*) therefore, there is no need to mention this leaf in the statement of signing:

» [$2 signed].

§8.3 Tanselle: A–C^4 D^4(**D4+1**) E–M^4.

» *Signatures:* $1–2; D4(1)=D5.
The actual signature of the insertion is ignored in favour of the positional indicator **+1**. The signature of the insertion is reported in the statement of signing.

§8.4 Bowers: A–C^4 D^4(**D3+'D4'**) E–M^4.

In gathering **D**, a leaf signed **D4** is inserted after **D3**. The collation makes it clear that the insertion **D4** is signed, by quoting it; therefore, there is no need to mention this leaf in the statement of signing:

» [$2 signed].

§8.5 Tanselle: A–C^4 D^4(**D3+1**) E–M^4.

» *Signatures:* $1–2; D3(1)=D4.

The actual signature of the insertion is ignored in favour of the positional indicator **+1**. The signature of the insertion is reported in the statement of signing.

§8.6 **Bowers:** A–C^4 **D^4(D2+d^2)** E–M^4.

In gathering **D**, a bifolium with its first leaf signed **d** is inserted after **D2**. The collation makes it clear that **d1** is signed but is silent about the signature of its conjugate leaf.

» *Second inserted leaf* signed: [$2+D[d2]) signed].
Although the second leaf of the inserted bifolium is signed (and therefore covered by the '$2 signed' statement), it must be mentioned, because it is an *insertion* (not a regular signing) the signing of which is not made evident in the collation.

» *Second inserted leaf* unsigned: [$2(–D[d2]) signed].

§8.7 **Tanselle:** A–C^4 D^4**(D2+1.2)** E–M^4.

The actual signatures of the inserted bifolium are ignored in favour of the positional indicator **+1.2**. The statement of signing will report which (if any) of the inserts are signed.

» *First and second inserted leaves* signed: *Signatures:* $1–2; D2(1)=d, D2(2)=d2.

» *First inserted leaf* signed, *second inserted leaf* unsigned: *Signatures:* $1–2; D2(1)=d.

§8.8 **Bowers:** A–C^4 D^4**(D1+*D^2)** E–M^4

In gathering **D**, a bifolium with its first leaf signed ***D** is inserted after **D1**. The collation makes it clear that ***D1** *is* signed but is silent about the signature of its conjugate leaf.

» *Second inserted leaf* signed: [$2(+D[*D2]) signed].
Although the second leaf of the inserted bifolium is signed (and therefore covered by the '$2 signed' statement), it must be mentioned, because it is an *insertion* (not a regular signing) the signing of which is not made evident in the collation.

» *Second inserted leaf* unsigned: [$2(–D[*D2]) signed].

§8.9 **Tanselle:** A–C^4 **D^4(D1+1.2)** E–M^4.

The actual signature of the inserted bifolium is ignored in favour of the positional indicator **+1.2**. The statement of signing will report which (if any) of the inserts are signed.

» *First and second inserted leaves* signed: *Signatures:* $1–2; D2(1)=*D, D2(2)=*D2.

» *First inserted leaf* signed, *second inserted leaf* unsigned: *Signatures:* $1–2; D2(1)=*D.

C. *McCristal's technique.*

Penny McCristal devised a useful shorthand for stating that half the leaves in a gathering are signed i.e., the employment of the fraction '½' as an index after the dollar sign.[15]

For example, the statement:

» A–K^8 L^4 [$^{½} signed (–A3)]

means that half the leaves of each gathering are signed. This is an accurate and succinct alternative to the traditional

» [$4 signed (–A3, L3, L4)].

[15] Penny McCristal, "'$½' as a Statement of Signing," *Bibliographical Society of Australia and New Zealand Bulletin* 19 (1995): 209-12.

§9 PUNCTUATION

Bowers favours a minimum of punctuation in the collation. He recommends placing a *comma*:

- between distinct alphabets:
  » (§^{2} a–d^4, B–K^4)
- after incomplete alphabets:
  » ¶^{2} A–L^4, 2A–2K^4
- after a long run of arbitrary marks:
  » ¶^{2} 2¶–3¶^{4} 4¶1, A–L^4.

A *comma* may also be employed whenever it would make the collation clearer.

He recommends using a *semicolon*:

- when the first item of a repeated alphabet has both a prefixed and a suffixed index number:
  » §^{2} A–K^4; ^{2}**A**^{2} B–V^4
- if a semicolon is necessary to separate these major series, the semicolon replaces the comma in separating all series:
  » π^2 A–T^4; 2A–3H^4 χ^2; ^{2}A–M^4; ^{3}A^2 B–X^4.

Complete agreement on the subject of punctuation has never been reached and the practice among bibliographers varies.

§10 PAGINATION AND FOLIATION

Books are *foliated* when the leaves are numbered (ff. 1–80). Books are *paginated* when the pages are numbered (pp. 1–160).

Preceding the statement of foliation or pagination is a note on the total number of leaves in the book. This note is a useful check, because there has to be agreement between the number of leaves expressed in the collation *and* the foliation or pagination statement; the number of pages must equal twice the number of leaves. For example, in the following collation:

> π^4 A–H^4 I^2 [\$$^{1/2}$ signed], 38 leaves, pp. [*4*] [i–v] vi-xi [xii], 1–60

the various segments tally with each other:

- number of leaves as expressed by the signatures: 4 + (8×4) + 2 = 38
- number of pages: 4 + 12 + 60 = 76
- 76 pages ÷ 2 = 38 leaves.

The statement of foliation or pagination can be part of the collational formula line, or it can be given in a separate paragraph.

There are many ways of expressing the foliation or pagination. I have limited my examples mainly to the style recommended by Bowers. I am illustrating bibliographical usage only and I acknowledge that library cataloguing practices may be in conflict.

Books without foliation or pagination.

» *Bowers:* 40 leaves unnumbered.

» *Alternative:* ff. [40].

» *Alternative:* 40 leaves, unnumbered [pp. 1–80].

Unnumbered and uncounted leaves or pages.

Preliminary: their total is given in italic within brackets; no attempt is made to infer any complete preliminary sequence.

» Bowers: pp. [*4*] 1–120.

Internal: their total is given in italic within brackets; no attempt is made to infer any complete internal sequence.

» Bowers: pp. 1–80 [*4*] 81–120.

Final: their numbering is inferred in roman within brackets.

» *Bowers (preferred)*: pp. 1–120 [121-128].

» *Bowers (alternative)*: pp 1–120 [*8*].

The final unnumbered sequence is not inferred and is given in italic, as a total, within brackets.

Unnumbered but counted leaves or pages.

Beginning and end of a sequence: their numbering is inferred in roman within brackets.

» *Bowers:* pp. **[i]** ii–x **[xi–xii]**, **[1]** 2–120.

Internal sequences: their numbering is inferred in roman within brackets.

» *Bowers:* pp. 1–80 **[81–82]** 83–120.

» *Alternative:* pp. 1–120.

The unnumbered pages or leaves are reported in a note.

Disturbances affecting the correctness of the printer's system of numeration.

A bracketed note for the correct total of the series affected must be provided at the end of that series.

» *Bowers:* pp. i–ix xi–xv [=**14**], 1–20 22–120 [=**118**].

» *Bowers (preferred):* pp. 1–20 22–120 [121–128] [=**126**].
The final inferred bracketed sequence ([121–128]) is included in the correct total of the series.

» *Bowers (alternative):* pp. 1–20 22–120 [=**118**] [*8*].
The final uninferred bracketed sequence ([**8**]) is not part of the preceding series.

Simple insertion, or cancellation followed by greater substitution.

In cases such as these, when repeated numbering may be introduced, Bowers suggests adopting a pagination formula closely tied to the signature formula. So, if the signatures read
A^4 B–Q^2 S–T^2 $V^2(V1+X^2)$
where:
A^4 = pp. [8] ; B–V1 = pp. 1–70 ; X^2 = pp. 71–74 ; V2 = pp. 71–72:

» *Bowers (preferred):* pp. [8] 1–70 71–74 71–72 [=76].

» *Bowers (alternative):* pp. [8] 1–74 71–72 [=76].

Books with both pagination and foliation.

» *Bowers:* pp. [2] [i] ii-vi; ff. [1] 2–35 [36].

Books numbered in whole or part by columns instead of by leaves or pages.

» *Bowers:* ff. [*1*]; cols. 1–56 [=39 ff.].
» *Bowers:* pp. [*2*] i–vi; cols. 1–140 [=70 pp.].

Books where sections are individually numbered.

» *Bowers:* pp. [*4*] i–xii, 1–290; ^{2}1–266; ^{3}[*4*] 1–262 [263–268].

The principle of the prefixed index is identical with that employed for duplicated signings of series (*Section 3C*). The aim in both cases is ease of reference.

§11 QUICK REFERENCE GUIDE TO THE COLLATION

In this *Quick Reference Guide* only the main points of collation-writing are outlined.

A. *Normal Gatherings.*

(a) Single signings.

§11.1 A–Z^{8}.

The order of signatures is that of the 23-letter Latin alphabet (which omits J, U, W). The letters J and U are sometimes used instead of the letters I and V, but this requires no comment as we are still dealing with a 23-letter alphabet. In the formula above, therefore, the signatures of the 9th and 20th gatherings could be either I or J, or U *or* V—but not both together!

§11.2 A–H^{4} **J**^{2} K–T^{4} **U**^{2} X^{4}.

If the gatherings signed J and/or U are not part of a series, their actual signings (that is, J not I, and U not V) must be made explicit.

§11.3 A–V^{8} **W**^{8} X–Z^{8}.

Exceptionally, the extra letter W was used. The presence of a gathering signed W must always be made explicit.

§11.4 1–6^{8} 7^{4}.

Gatherings signed with numbers instead of letters.

§11.5 [A]^{4} *or* (A)^{4} = A^{4}.

Brackets or parentheses around signatures are ignored but may be the subject of a note.

§11.6 a^{4} $\mathfrak{A}^{4}$ $\mathfrak{B}^{4}$ c^{2} = a^{4} A–B^{4} C^{2}.

The collation is always written in roman. Small capitals are rendered as capitals.

§11.8 A–D^{4}.

Unbroken sequences of letters in the same case (upper-case or lower-case) and with the same index number, can be joined with a dash.

§11.9 a–b^{4}, A–D^{4}.

Sequences of letters in different cases need to be distinguished.

§11.10 A–B^{4} D–F^{4}.

Broken sequence of letters.

§11.11 ✠^{2} ¶^{2} §^{2} B–K^{4}.

Unless arbitrary marks constitute a sequence, each must be noted by its own index number.

§11.12 **¶–3¶**^{2} A–F^{4}.

Doubled, tripled, etc. arbitrary marks are expressed by adding an appropriate prefixed number to them.

(b) Doubled and other multiple signings.

§11.13 A–Y^{8} 2A–2M^{8} 2N^{4} 3A–3Y^{8} 4A–4E^{8}.

Doubled, tripled, etc. signatures (Aa, Aaa, etc.) are expressed by replacing them with an appropriate prefixed number.

(c) Duplicated signings.

§11.14 A–2M^{4}, ^{2}A–Y^{4}, ^{3}A–2Z^{4}.

An appropriate index number is prefixed to the letters of the duplicated signings and included when quoting.

B. *Inferred Signings.*

Examples of inference.

§11.15 **[unsigned gathering]**^{4} B–X^{4}.

» *Bowers:* [A]^{4} B–X^{4}.

The first gathering of the book is inferred as **A**.

» *Alternative:* π^4 B–X^4.

§11.16 ¶^{2} [unsigned section title-gathering]^2 B–M^4.

» *Bowers and Structural approach:* ¶^{2} [A]^2 B–M^4.
Bowers would infer an unsigned gathering which is not the first gathering of a book as **A** only if it were a title-gathering or a section title-gathering. The structural approach, on the other hand, focuses on *position* only: the unsigned gathering can be inferred as **A** whether it is a title-gathering or not.

» *Alternative:* π^2 ¶^{2} B–M^4.

§11.17 A–E^4 [F]^2 G–T^4.

Single inference in the body of the text.

§11.18 A–D^4 [E–F]^4 G^2.

Two consecutive inferences in the body of the text.

§11.19 ¶^{4} [2¶]^4 A–X^4.

Arbitrary marks can be inferred.

» *Bowers (alternative):* ¶^{4} π^4 A–X^4.

§11.20 A–T^4 [V]^4.

Unsigned final gatherings may be inferred if they contain the conclusion of the text (see also *Example §11.27*).

C. *The Symbols π and χ.*

(a) The symbol π.

The symbol π is used for unsigned and uninferrable *prefixed* gatherings; that is, gatherings preceding the first letter, actual or inferred, of the *main* alphabetical sequence.

§11.21 [unsigned gathering]^2 A–D^4.

» π^2 A–D^4.

§11.22 ¶^{4} [unsigned gathering]^2 A–V^4.

» *Bowers (preferred):* ¶^{4} [2¶]^2 A–V^4.
Bowers prefers inference where attainable.

» *Bowers (alternative):* ¶^{4} π^2 A–V^4.

§11.23 [unsigned gathering]^2 ¶^{4} [unsigned gathering]^2 B–Y^4.

» *Bowers:* [A]^2 ¶^{4} [2¶]^2 B–Y^4.

» *Alternative:* π^2 ¶^{4} 2π^2 B–Y^4.

» *Structural approach:* π^2 ¶^{4} [A]^2 B–Y^4.

§11.24 [unsigned gathering]^4 *^{4} C–X^4.

» *Bowers:* π^4 *^{4} C–X^4.
The unsigned gathering cannot be inferred as **A** because there is no gathering **B** to link it gathering **C**.

§11.25 [unsigned gathering]^2 a–q^4, B–X^4.

» *Bowers (preferred):* π^2 a–q^4, B–X^4 .
The unsigned title-gathering is not inferred because it is many gatherings away from gathering **B**.

» *Bowers (alternative):* [A]^2, a–q^4, B–X^4.

(b) The symbol χ.

The symbol χ is used for unsigned and uninferrable gatherings which are not prefixed.

§11.26 [unsigned title-gathering]^2 ¶^{2} [unsigned gathering]^2 B–M^4.

» *Bowers (preferred)*: [A]^2 ¶^{2} [2¶]^2 B–M^4.
Bowers prefers inference where attainable.

» *Bowers (alternative):* [A]^2 ¶^{2} χ^2 B–M^4.
The symbol χ *can* be admitted in the preliminaries for an unsigned and uninferrable gathering which is not prefixed.

» *Conservative approach:* π^2 ¶^{2} 2π^2 B–M^4.

§11.27 A–T^4 χ^4.

Unsigned final gatherings are not inferred if they contain only ambiguous leaves such as errata leaves, advertisements, etc. (see also *Example §11.20*)

§11.28 A–B^4 χ^2 C–K^4.

The unsigned gathering cannot be inferred because there is no gap in the alphabetical sequence.

§11.29 **[unsigned gathering]^2 [unsigned gathering]^4** B–Y^4.

» *Bowers:* [A]^2 χ^4 B–Y^4.

» *Structural approach:* π^2 [A]^4 B–Y^4.

(c) Using more than one π or χ symbol.

The symbols π and χ can be doubled, tripled, etc.

§11.30 π–2π^2 A–V^4.

and

§11.31 A–D^4 χ-2χ^2 E–V^4.

(d) π as a prefixed superior index symbol.

When a *prefixed* leaf, gathering, or series exhibits the same system of signing as the regular signed ones, the symbol π can be employed to ensure precise referencing (as a prefixed index symbol).

§11.32 $^{\pi}$**A**^{4} a–f^4, A–M^6 *not* A^4 a–f^4, ^{2}A–M^6.

The index number 2 is employed only for duplicated signings; in this case the main alphabetical series is A–M^6.

(e) χ as a prefixed index symbol.

When a *non-prefixed* leaf, gathering, or series bears the same system of signing as the regular signed ones, the symbol χ can be employed to ensure precise referencing (as a prefixed index symbol).

§11.33 A^4 ¶^{2} B–C^4 $^{\chi}$**D**^{4} D^4 $^{\chi}$¶^{2} E–F^4.

D. *Insertions.*

(a) Separate (disjunct) leaves outside the gathering.

(i) *Insertions not associated with the preceding or succeeding gathering.*

It is advisable to treat an unsigned leaf, fold, or series of leaves between gatherings as a separate item. It is *not* customary to associate a final unsigned leaf or leaves with the preceding gathering.

§11.34 A–C^4 **χ1** D–L^4 **[M]1** N–P^4 **2χ^2**

(ii) *Insertions associated in signing or direction-numbering with the preceding gathering.*

A single leaf or disjunct leaves at the end of a gathering are considered to belong to the preceding gathering only when they are associated to it in their signing or direction-numbering.

§11.35 A–B^4 C^4 **[leaf signed C5]** D^4

» *Bowers:* A–B^4 C^4(C4+C5) D^4.
C5 is signed but there is no need to quote it.

» *No association:* A–B^4 C^4 $^{\chi}$C1 D^4.
The actual signing of the insertion is reported in the statement of signing.

§11.36 A–B^4 C^4 **[leaf signed *C5]** D^4.

» *Bowers:* A–B^4 C^4(C4+*C5) D^4.
Leaf *C5 is signed but there is no need to quote it.

» *No association:* A–C^4 $^{\chi}$C1 D^4.
The actual signing of the insertion is reported in the statement of signing.

§11.37 A–B^4 C^4 **[leaf direction-numbered 5]** D^4.

» *Bowers:* A–B^4 C^4(C4+'5') D^4.
Quoting the direction-number is essential.

» *No association:* A–C^4 χ1 D^4.
The actual direction number of the insertion is reported in the statement of signing: χ1 direction-numbered '5'.

§11.38 A–B^4 C^4 [leaf signed C5] [unsigned leaf] [unsigned leaf] D^4.

- » *Bowers (preferred):* A–B^4 C^4(C4+'C5',C6,C7) D^4.
  Leaf C5 is signed; the two disjunct leaves following it can be inferred as C6 and C7 because leaf 'C5' provides the peg on which to hang the inference, and because of their ultimate and unambiguous position.
- » *Bowers (alternative):* A–B^4 C^4(C4+'C5',χ1,2) D^4.
- » *Bowers (alternative):* A–B^4 C^4(C4+C5+2) D^4.
- » *No association:* A–B^4 C^4 $^{\chi}$C1 χ1 2χ1 D^4.
  The actual signing of the insertion is reported in the statement of signing.

(iii) *Insertions associated in signing or direction-numbering with the succeeding gathering.*

These types of insertion are better treated as 'not associated'.

§11.39 A–C^4 [leaf signed D] D^4 E^4.

- » *Bowers:* A–C^4 $^{\chi}$D1 D^4 E^4.
- » *Alternative:* A–C^4 D^4('D1'+D1) E^4.
  With this technique the signature of the insertion must always to be quoted.

(b) Separate (disjunct) leaves *inside* the gathering.

§11.40 A–B^4 [C1 C2 C3 [leaf signed C4] C^4] D^4.

- » *Bowers:* A–B^4 C^4(C3+'C4') D^4.
  The signature of the insertion must be quoted because it duplicates the regular C4 signing.
- » *Tanselle:* A–B^4 C^4(C3+1) D^4.

§11.41 A–B^4 [C1 C2 C3 [unsigned leaf] C^4] D^4.

- » *Bowers (preferred):* A–B^4 C^4(C3+χ1) D^4.
- » *Bowers (alternative):* A–B^4 C^4(C3+1) D^4.
- » *Tanselle:* A–B^4 C^4(C3+1) D^4.
  Rejection of the use of the symbol χ for insertions inside the gathering.

§11.42 A–B^4 [C1 C2 C3 [leaf signed C4] [unsigned leaf] C4] D^4.

- » *Bowers (preferred):* A–B^4 C^4(C3+'C4',χ1) D^4.
  The unsigned disjunct leaf is not inferred: refusal to perpetuate inferentially an anomalous signing.

- » *Bowers (alternative):* A–B^4 C^4(C3+'C4'+1) D^4.

- » *Tanselle:* A–B^4 C^4(C3+1,2) D^4.
  Rejection of the use of the symbol χ for insertions.

(c) Folds *outside* the gathering.

(i) *Folds, either unsigned, or signed on the first leaf with a presumed '1'.*

These types of insertions are treated as separate gatherings.

§11.43 A–D^4 ***D^2** E^4 *and* A–D^4 $^{\chi}$**D^2** E^4.

and

§11.44 A–D^4 χ^4 E^4.

(ii) *Signed folds continuing or duplicating the numbering of a preceding gathering.*

§11.45 A–C^4 D^4 **[leaf signed D4].[unsigned leaf].[unsigned leaf].[unsigned leaf]** E^4.

- » *Bowers:* A–C^4 D^4(D4+'D4'.5.6.7) E^4.
  The insertion D4 is signed, and the following three leaves can be inferred as D5, D6, D7 because they together form a pair of quired bifolia ('D4' providing the peg for inference), and because of their ultimate and unambiguous position.

- » *No association:* A–D^4 $^{\chi}$D^4 E^4.
  The actual signing of the insertion is reported in the statement of signing.

§11.46 A–C^4 D^4 **[leaf signed *D5] [leaf signed *D6].[unsigned leaf]** E^4.

- » *Bowers:* A–C^4 D^4(D4+*D5,*D6.7) E^4.
  The leaf following *D6 (the peg for inference) can be inferred as *D7 because it is conjugate with it and because of its ultimate and unambiguous position.

- » *No association:* A–D^4 *D1 $^{\chi}$*D^2 E^4.
  The actual signings of the insertions are reported in the statement of signing.

(d) Folds *inside* the gathering.

(i) *Folds signed on the first leaf with a number other than '1'.*

§11.47 A–D^4 [E1 **[leaf signed E2].[unsigned leaf]** E2 E3 E4] F^4.

» *Bowers:* A–D^4 E^4(E1+'E2'.1) F^4.
The insertion signed E2 needs to be quoted to differentiate it from the regular E2 signing. The signature of the unsigned leaf is not inferred: refusal to perpetuate inferentially an anomalous signing.

» *Tanselle:* A–D^4 E^4(E1+1.2) F^4.
The actual signing of the insertion (replaced by the positional indicator +1) is reported in the statement of signing.

(ii) *Folds signed on the first leaf with a presumed '1'.*

§11.48 A–C^4 [D1 **[leaf signed *D].[unsigned leaf]** D3 D4] E–F^4.

» *Bowers (preferred):* A–C^4 D^4(D1+*D^2) E–F^4.
Leaf *D1 is signed. The statement of signing will make it clear whether leaf *D2 is signed or not.

» *Bowers (alternative):* A–C^4 D^4(D1+*D1.2) E–F^4.

» *Tanselle:* A–C^4 D^4(D1+1.2) E–F^4.
The actual signing of the insertion (replaced by the positional indicator +1) is reported in the statement of signing.

§11.49 A–C^4 [D1 D2 **[unsigned leaf].[unsigned leaf]** D3 D4] E–F^4.

» *Bowers (preferred):* A–C^4 D^4(D2+χ^2) E–F^4.
χ must be used for the unsigned bifolium as no inference is possible.

» *Bowers (alternative):* A–C^4 D^4(D2+1.2) E–F^4.

» *Tanselle:* A–C^4 D^4(D2+1.2) E–F^4.
Rejection of the use of the symbol χ for insertions.

E. *Cancellation and Substitution.*

(a) Simple cancellation.

§11.50 A–B^4 C^4(**–C2**).

Leaf C2 has been excised.

§11.51 A–B^4 C^4(**–C1,2**).

Disjunct leaves C1 and C2 have been excised.

§11.52 A–B^4 C^4(**–C1.4**).

Conjugate leaves C1 and C4 have been excised.

(b) Cancellation and substitution of *equal* number of leaves at the same places in the gathering.

(i) *Cancellation followed by insertion expressed with the ± symbol.*

§11.53 A–B^4 C^4(**±C3**) D^4(**±D2,4**) E–I^4 K^4(**±K2.3**) L^4(**±**).

Bowers encourages a very free inference when the ± symbol is employed, dropping quoting altogether.

- Cancellandum C3 has been replaced by cancellans C3.
- Disjunct cancellanda D2 and D4 have been replaced by disjunct cancellantia D2 and D4.
- Conjugate cancellanda K2 and K3 have been replaced by conjugate cancellantia K2 and K3.
- Cancellandum gathering L of four leaves has been replaced by a cancellans gathering L of four leaves of normal conjugacy.

(i) *Cancellation followed by insertion expressed with the plus (+) and minus (–) signs in an expanded formula.*

§11.54 A–B^4 C^4(**–C3,4+C3.4**) D^4.

Cancellation and substitution of the same number of leaves, in the same position, but with different conjugacy.

§11.55 A–B^4 [C1 C2 C3 ~~C4~~ **c4**] D^4.

» *Bowers:* A–B^4 C^4(–C4+c4) D^4.
The ± symbol cannot be used because cancellandum C4 belongs to a gathering signed in upper-case, whereas cancellans c4 is signed in lower-case.

» *Tanselle:* A–B^4 C^4(±C4) D^4.
A note in the statement of signing is required: C4 = c4.

§11.56 A–B^4 [~~C1~~ ~~C2~~ ***C.[unsigned leaf]** D^4.

» *Bowers (preferred)***:** A–B^4 C^4(–C1,2+*C^2) D^4.
The ± symbol cannot be used because a conjugate pair (*C^2) has replaced a disjunct pair (C1,2). The statement of signing will make it clear that the leaf conjugate with leaf ***C1** is *not* signed.

» *Bowers (alternative):* A–B^4 C^4(–C1,2+*C1.2) D^4.

(c) Cancellation and substitution of *different* number of leaves starting at the same place in the gathering.

§11.57 A^4 [B1 B2 B3 ~~B4~~ **B4 [unsigned leaf]**] C^4.

The principles governing simple insertion apply.

» *Bowers (preferred):* A^4 B^4(–B4+'B4',B5) C^4.

» *Bowers (alternative):* A^4 B^4(±B4+1) C^4.

» *Tanselle:* A^4 B^4(±B4+1) C^4.

§11.58 A^4 [B1 B2 ~~B3~~ **B3 [unsigned leaf]** B4] C^4.

» *Bowers (preferred):* A^4 B^4(–B3+'B3',χ1) C^4.
The unsigned insertion cannot be inferred as B4 because that would duplicate the regular B4 signing: refusal to perpetuate inferentially an anomalous signing.

» *Bowers (alternative):* A^4 B^4(±B3+1) C^4.

» *Tanselle:* A^4 B^4(±B3+1) C^4.

§11.59 A^4 [B1 B2 ~~B3~~ **B3.[unsigned leaf]** B4] C^4.

» *Bowers:* A^4 B^4(–B3+'B3'.1) C^4.
The unsigned insertion cannot be inferred as B4 because that would duplicate the regular B4 signing: refusal to perpetuate inferentially an anomalous signing.

» *Tanselle:* A^4 B^4(–B3+1.2) C^4.

§11.60 A^4 [B1 B2 ~~B3~~ **[unsigned leaf].[unsigned leaf]** B4] C^4.

» *Bowers:* A^4 B^4(–B3+χ^2) C^4.
The two unsigned leaves cannot be inferred because there is no peg on which to hang the inference.

» *Tanselle:* A^4 B^4(–B3+1.2) C^4.

§11.61 A^4 [~~B1~~ **B1.[signed or unsigned leaf]** B2 B3 B4] C^4.

» *Bowers (preferred):* A^4 B^4(–B1+B^2) C^4.
The statement of signing will make it clear whether the leaf conjugate with leaf B(B1) is signed or not.

» *Bowers (alternative):* A^4 B^4(–B1+B1.2) C^4.

» *Tanselle:* A^4 B^4(–B1+1.2) C^4.

(d) Insertion and cancellation occurring at different places in the same gathering.

§11.62 A^4 [B1 ~~B2~~ **B2** B3 **B4** B4] C^4.

» *Bowers:* A^4 B^4(B3+'B4'; –B2) C^4.
Bowers prefers to start the collation with the plus sign (+).

» *Alternative:* A^4 B^4(–B2; B3+'B4') C^4.
Some writers prefer to start the collation with the minus sign (–).

BIBLIOGRAPHY

Bowers, Fredson. "Format and Collational Formula," "Reference Notation," "Statement of Signing; Pagination and Foliation", "A digest of the Formulary." Chap. 5, 6, 7, Appendix 1 in *Principles of Bibliographical Description*. Princeton: Princeton University Press, 1949.

Gaskell, Philip. "Bibliographical Description," in *A New Introduction to Bibliography*. Oxford: Oxford University Press, 1974.

Greg, W. W. "A Formulary of Collation." *Library* 4th ser., 14 (1933-34): 365-82.

McCristal, Penny. "'$½' as a Statement of Signing." *Bibliographical Society of Australia and New Zealand Bulletin* 19 (1995): 209-12.

McKerrow, Ronald B. "Some Points of Bibliographical Technique. The Description of a Book. References to Passages in Early Books." Part 2, Chap. 1 in *An Introduction to Bibliography for Literary Students*. Oxford: Clarendon Press, 1928.

McMullin, B. J. "The Description of Volumes Gathered in Nines." *Script & Print* 37 (2013): 32-39.

———. Treatment of insertions in the collation formula. In "Bowers's Principles of Bibliographical Description." *Bibliographical Society of Australia and New Zealand Bulletin* 15 (1991): 57-58.

Needham, Paul. *The Bradshaw Method: Henry Bradshaw's Contribution to Bibliography*. Chapel Hill, NC: Hanes Foundation, 1988.

Padwick, E.W. "Bibliographical Description (2). Collation Paragraph." In *Bibliographical Method*. Cambridge: James Clarke, 1969.

Pearce, M.J. "Collation and Colophon," in *Workbook of Analytical & Descriptive Bibliography*. London: Bingley, 1970.

Spedding, Patrick. "Cancelled Errata in *John Buncle, Junior, Gentleman*." *Script & Print* 38 (2014): 115-21. See also "Responses to Patrick Spedding, 'Cancelled Errata in John Buncle, Junior, Gentleman'." *Script & Print* 38 (2014): 249-52.

Tanselle, G. Thomas. "Title-Page Transcription and Signature Collation Reconsidered." *Studies in Bibliography* 38 (1985): 45-81.

ACKNOWLEDGEMENTS

I wish to thank, first and foremost, Brian McMullin without whose help, both scholarly and practical, this book could not have been written.

Thanks are also due to Ann McDermott (British Library) and Andrea Del Cornò (London Library) for their many comments and suggestions, and to Caren Florance who, with angelic patience and devilish professionalism, has turned a mangled text into a book.

ABOUT THE AUTHOR

Carlo Dumontet is an independent bibliographer, formerly of the National Art Library, Victoria & Albert Museum, London.

Milton Keynes UK
Ingram Content Group UK Ltd.
UKHW051644081024
449373UK00019B/299